The Complete Dismissal Package

THE COMPLEMENTARY WEBSITE

The http://books.indicator.co.uk website gives you instant access to all the ready-to-use documents, tools, policies, etc. that complement this publication.

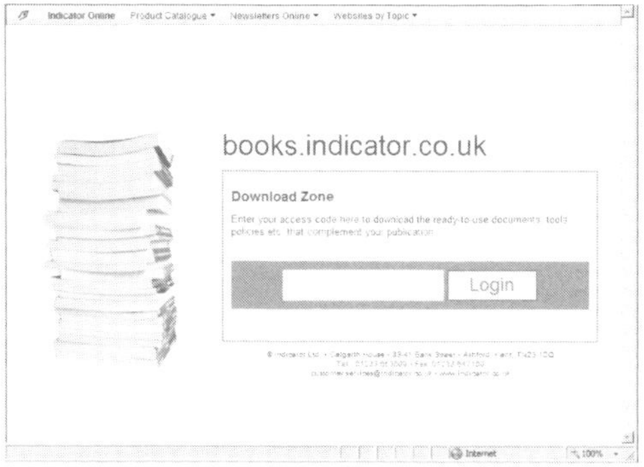

Go to

http://books.indicator.co.uk

THE CD-ROM

Don't have access to the Internet?
Call Customer Services on 01233 653500 to request a CD-ROM.

We have made every effort to ensure that the information contained in this book reflects the law as at September 1 2010.

Where the male pronoun has been used this is simply to avoid cumbersome language and no discrimination or bias is intended.

Likewise, where the word spouse is mentioned, this also refers to a civil partner.

ISBN 978-1-906892-25-8

First Edition - First print - E01P1

Every effort has been made by Indicator Limited to ensure that the information given is accurate and not misleading, but Indicator Limited cannot accept responsibility for any loss or liability perceived to have arisen from the use of any such information. Only Acts of Parliament and Statutory Instruments have the force of law and only the courts can authoritatively interpret the law.

Introduction

Every employer knows the importance of following a good disciplinary and dismissal procedure. Long gone are the hire and fire days. Make a mistake and a savvy employee (or their trade union) will have you before an employment tribunal quicker than you can say "what's it worth?". Trouble is, it's difficult to find quality information and practical advice on all the stages leading up to and following dismissal. Although the ACAS Code of Practice which came into effect in April 2009 was supposed to simplify matters, in fact, the reverse has happened. So we decided to put together a book that details every intricate element of the dismissal process. It's split into three parts: understanding and following the ACAS Code of Practice; how to use workplace mediation and, if the dispute does end up in a claim, how to get to grips with employment tribunal procedure.

Written in easy to understand language, and full of highly practical tips for employers, it should be all you need to play it safe and ensure that even if a troublesome employee does issue tribunal papers, you'll be fully equipped to deal with the claim in a sensible, cost-effective way.

Duncan Callow
September 2010

Table of contents

Chapter 1 - Disciplinary and grievance procedures

Chapter 2 - Mediation and the new ACAS Code of Practice

Chapter 3 - Avoiding and managing employment tribunal claims

Chapter 4 - Documents

CHAPTER 1

Disciplinary and grievance procedures

1.1. WHAT'S HAPPENED TO THE STATUTORY PROCEDURES?

On April 6 2009 the statutory disciplinary, dismissal and grievance procedures were abolished. When they were originally introduced in 2004, it was said that they would vastly improve the way workplace disputes were handled. However, this has proved not to be the case.

After much criticism, the government commissioned Michael Gibbons to examine the statutory regime with the purpose of seeing if it could be simplified and improved, whilst still preserving employee rights. What followed became known as the "Gibbons Review". It recommended the abolition of the statutory procedures, which the government chose to implement under the **Employment Act 2008**.

1.1.1. Why were they abolished?

Depending on the circumstances, the statutory procedures made it compulsory for employers to follow either a standard three-step or modified two-step procedure. If an employer failed to do so and went on to dismiss an employee, the dismissal would be "automatically unfair". It was believed that if employers were forced to try to resolve issues using standard procedures, there would be far fewer tribunal claims. In particular, it was suggested that employees who were merely disgruntled, as opposed to wronged in some way, would be deterred from issuing claims against their employer. This proposal was supposed to halt the clogging-up of an already stretched tribunal system. This was a great theory but when it was put into practice it didn't work.

Despite assurances to the contrary, the statutory procedures failed businesses badly. Although both the standard and modified procedures initially appeared to be simple to follow, the reality for employers was very different. In 2007, two years after their introduction, the Federation of Small Businesses conducted a survey of 3,000 businesses: 65% of them thought the statutory procedures were the most burdensome of all employment legislation.

Not only did they cause widespread confusion, they actually led to an increase in claims. Employment tribunal statistics show that in 2006/7 132,577 claims were dealt with, compared to 115,039 in 2005/6. As the statutory procedures were so vague, a large number of these cases were brought to clarify their meaning. Another criticism was that they were centred on the tribunal process, which was becoming increasingly legalistic. This meant employers had to not only place greater reliance on the use of lawyers and employment specialists, but also incur their fees. This defeated the objective of the tribunal system that was originally set up to offer a fast and simple solution to employment disputes. So what was meant to be a cost-effective system was spiralling out of control.

1.1.2. What has taken their place?

The statutory procedures have been replaced by a new **ACAS Code of Practice - Disciplinary and Grievance Procedures** (the Code). It provides practical guidance on how workplace disciplinary issues and grievances should be handled once the statutory procedures go. Whilst there's no legal requirement to follow the Code, tribunals will take it into account when considering the merits of a case. To supplement the Code, ACAS has produced guidance entitled *"Discipline and Grievances at Work: The ACAS Guide"*. But unlike the Code, tribunals don't have to give any consideration to its contents when dealing with cases (see later).

Download Zone

For the **ACAS Code of Practice**, visit **http://books.indicator.co.uk**. You'll find the access code on page 2 of this book.

1.1.3. What are the key changes?

The Code differs from the statutory regime in two respects. Firstly, less emphasis is placed on the mechanics of managing disciplinary issues, grievances and dismissals. Instead, the focus is on fairness. Also there's greater flexibility afforded to both sides, so problems should be resolved earlier on. However, the statutory procedures can't be entirely consigned to history, as you're encouraged to continue to follow the general principles laid down by them in order to achieve a fair process.

Several key changes are introduced by the Code:

- a dismissal is no longer "automatically unfair" simply because an employer fails to follow the Code
- the option to extend time limits on procedures is removed
- there's no longer a modified procedure
- employers are only required to issue a first and then final written warning prior to dismissing an employee
- there's now no mention of verbal warnings
- an employee is not required to raise a formal grievance prior to lodging a tribunal claim
- both employers and employees can be penalised if they unreasonably fail to follow the Code by an adjustment of up to 25% on any compensatory award. Under the statutory procedures awards could be adjusted by 10-50% but only in the employee's favour
- should an employee raise a grievance that's linked to a disciplinary issue, it can now be dealt with concurrently. The disciplinary procedure doesn't have to be halted in order to deal with the grievance

- there's now an acknowledgement that smaller businesses may not be able to incorporate all the elements of the Code into their procedures. Under the previous regime, all businesses were required to follow the minimum statutory disciplinary and dismissal procedures
- it doesn't apply to redundancies or the termination of fixed-term contracts
- mediation is actively promoted as a way of resolving workplace disputes.

Employer tip

Don't be tempted to throw out your existing disciplinary and grievance procedures: elements of the statutory procedures will still need to be followed.

Employer tip

The Code acknowledges that smaller businesses may not be able to implement all aspects of it, so use this to your advantage. Update disciplinary and grievance procedures in a way that best suits the needs of your business.

Key points

The statutory disciplinary and grievance procedures were:

- abolished on April 6 2009
- replaced by a new ACAS Code of Practice
- supplemented by new ACAS guidance.

They have been replaced because they:

- led to a rapid rise in the number of tribunal claims
- were too complex for many employers to understand
- made the tribunal system too costly for employers.

The key changes in the new Code are:

- if there's any failure to follow any part of the Code, any subsequent dismissal will no longer be "automatically unfair"
- the extension of time limits that currently apply to grievances and dismissals have been removed
- there's no longer a modified procedure
- verbal warnings aren't mentioned; only first and final written warnings
- there's no legal requirement for an employee to raise a formal grievance before lodging a claim in the tribunal
- if either party unreasonably fails to follow the Code, any awards may be adjusted by up to 25% either way
- when a grievance is raised that's linked to the disciplinary matter it can be dealt with concurrently
- it doesn't apply to redundancies or the termination of fixed-term contracts
- mediation is now actively encouraged to resolve workplace disputes.

The new ACAS Code of Practice:

- is more flexible and allows problems to be resolved earlier on
- takes into account the size and resources of the business
- recognises that smaller businesses may not be able to implement all its elements.

1.2. THE NEW ACAS CODE

1.2.1. What is the new ACAS Code of Practice?

It's a series of principles aimed at employers, employees and their representatives designed to help them resolve workplace disciplinary issues and grievances. At only ten pages long, the Code is much shorter than its statutory predecessor. It's flexible and can be used as a broad framework to create procedures, which work in a way that best suit your business.

1.2.2. What is its legal status?

There's no legal requirement for you to follow the Code. However, tribunals will take it into account when deciding on the merits of individual cases. In practice, this means that a tribunal will look more favourably on you if you've built the principles laid down in the Code into your disciplinary and grievance procedures, and can also demonstrate that you've taken reasonable steps to follow it.

Employer tip

The Code doesn't apply to the non-renewal of fixed-term contracts or to redundancy dismissals.

1.2.3. Is it good news?

You will certainly be better off under the Code and it's believed smaller businesses in particular will benefit from it. In addition, it applies equally to employees, unlike the statutory procedures, which were often abused by them. The fact that a dismissal won't be "automatically unfair" if you fail to follow the Code will benefit all employers, but particularly smaller ones which don't have dedicated departments dealing with employment matters.

Another plus is that tribunal awards can only be uplifted by a maximum of 25%. Tribunals had seemingly been following the statutory procedures to the letter and it was not uncommon for successful claimants to be awarded uplifts on compensation close to the permitted maximum of 50%.

However, tribunals are yet to interpret various elements of the Code and decide on what certain phrases mean. As an example, the meaning of *"unreasonable delay"* is currently undefined and still awaits clarification.

1.2.4. What could happen if we don't follow it?

Even though there can no longer be a finding of "automatically unfair dismissal", we would recommend that you follow the Code carefully. This is for two main reasons. Firstly, a tribunal can increase a compensation award by up to 25% for any unreasonable failure to follow it. Secondly, as the law will, in theory, revert to its pre-October 2004 position, the "Polkey principle" comes back into play. This principle established that the dismissal of an employee can be unfair simply because an employer failed to follow a fair dismissal procedure.

Tribunals can look closely at the following: **(1)** the individual chosen to conduct the disciplinary hearing, i.e. if they're different to the one carrying out the initial investigation; **(2)** the strength and reliability of the evidence; **(3)** how the evidence was assessed; and **(4)** the level of access the employee is given to the evidence against them.

Employer tip

The average tribunal compensation award is only £8,000 for an unfair dismissal claim. An uplift of 25% could make a serious difference to your bottom line in the current economic climate.

1.3. DISCIPLINARY MATTERS - THE CODE

1.3.1. What do we do first?

The Code states that an investigation into a possible or actual disciplinary matter must be undertaken without *"unreasonable delay"*. What this amounts to isn't yet defined, so there's currently some flexibility on the time frame, which will very much depend on individual circumstances, e.g. the availability of witnesses. If an investigation relates to alleged misconduct, it's recommended that the investigation and disciplinary hearings are carried out by different people (however, the Code recognises that this may not be practicable for small businesses). There's no statutory right for an employee to be accompanied to a formal investigatory meeting. That said, the overall principles of fairness and transparency will mean that in some cases a companion should be offered, e.g. for employees whose first language isn't English, those with hearing problems or those who have learning difficulties.

Employer tip

Irrespective of what the investigatory meeting is for, you still need to ensure that it doesn't accidentally turn into a disciplinary hearing.

Download Zone

For a **Disciplinary Procedure**, visit **http://books.indicator.co.uk**. You'll find the access code on page 2 of this book.

1.3.2. What happens if we decide on a disciplinary hearing?

If, following your investigation, you decide there's a need for a disciplinary hearing, you should notify the employee of this in writing. When doing so include the following information: **(1)** the reason(s) why disciplinary proceedings are being invoked; **(2)** the possible consequences for the employee; **(3)** copies of any written evidence, e.g. witness statements; **(4)** a reminder for the employee of their right to be accompanied; and **(5)** the date and time of the hearing.

Employer tip

As the Code is not legally binding, there's no law that prevents you from suspending an employee. So provided you've previously retained the contractual right to do so, you can continue with this practice.

Download Zone

For a **Notification of Disciplinary Hearing**, visit **http://books.indicator.co.uk**. You'll find the access code on page 2 of this book.

1.3.3. When can we start the disciplinary hearing?

The Code doesn't suggest a timeframe between an employer notifying an employee of a hearing and when it goes ahead. It simply states that an employee should have *"reasonable time"* to prepare their case for a meeting, which should be held *"without unreasonable delay"*. With regards to attendance it says, *"employers and employees (and their companions) should make every effort to attend the meeting"*.

1.3.4. Does the employee have a right to be accompanied at the hearing?

The employee's legal right to be accompanied has been transferred to the Code. So where the disciplinary meeting may lead to the: **(1)** issuing of a formal warning; **(2)** taking of some other disciplinary action; or **(3)** confirmation of a warning, the employee can have a companion present. The chosen companion may only be a colleague, union representative, or an official employed by a trade union. A companion is permitted to put the employee's case, respond on their behalf, confer with them during the hearing and sum up their evidence. However, they have no right to answer questions on the employee's behalf or address the hearing if the employee doesn't wish it.

Note. The employee's choice of companion must be a reasonable one. The Code gives two examples of when the choice of companion won't be reasonable, namely, where: **(1)** their presence would prejudice the hearing; or **(2)** they're selected from a geographically remote site.

1.3.5. What format should the hearing take?

Assuming that the employee has turned up (along with any companion), the hearing should follow a logical format. Begin by explaining the nature of the complaint and follow this by reviewing the evidence that has been collected. The employee should then be allowed to set out their case and respond to the allegations. They should also be given an opportunity to ask their own questions and call witnesses of their own.

EMPLOYER TIP

Use the flexibility of the Code to your advantage. Consider whether you could reasonably reduce the time period between notifying the employee of the hearing and it taking place, e.g. from five days to four. But do be prepared to make exceptions, e.g. if a vital witness is on leave.

1.3.6. What can we do if the employee doesn't show up?

There's no indication of what you should do in the event an employee doesn't show up to a meeting. The only ACAS guidance on this is at paragraph 24 of the Code which says: "*where an employee is persistently unable or unwilling to attend a disciplinary meeting without good cause, the employer should make a decision on the evidence available.*" This, of course, raises the question as to what "persistent" means, and is yet to be clarified by the Employment Appeal Tribunal (EAT).

EMPLOYER TIP

Until the meaning of "persistent" is clarified by the EAT, consider defining it as two no-shows; assuming you can demonstrate that this has happened without good reason. Amend your procedures so it's clear you'll proceed on the third occasion should an employee fail to attend earlier hearings.

1.3.7. What should we do after the hearing?

After the hearing you need to inform the employee of your decision in writing. The Code sets out what type of sanction is appropriate and how you should proceed:

- **First written warning.** This would be for a first act of misconduct or poor performance.

- **Final written warning.** This would be appropriate for a further act of misconduct, or for failing to improve performance within a given period of time. However, it can also be used where a first act of misconduct or unsatisfactory performance merits it, e.g. where the employee's action or performance has harmed your business, or has the potential to do so.
- **Dismissal.** There may be times where the wrongdoing is sufficiently serious so that dismissal on the grounds of gross misconduct is an appropriate response. The types of behaviour which qualify haven't changed under the Code: theft, fighting, working whilst under the influence of drink and drugs and violence are still covered (but this list is not exhaustive).

1.3.8. What do we need to consider when issuing a written warning?

When issuing a written warning, you still need to set out the nature of the misconduct or poor performance, which has led to disciplinary proceedings and how you expect the employee to respond and by when. Tell an employee how long a warning will remain in place and the likely sanctions they'll face if they don't make the necessary improvements, e.g. dismissal.

Employer tip

A decision to dismiss an employee should only be taken by a manager or individual with the express authority to do so.

Note. At the moment, paragraph 22 of the Code is contradictory. Whilst it acknowledges that incidences of gross misconduct will justify dismissal without notice for a first offence, it then goes on to state: *"a fair disciplinary process should always be followed, before dismissing for gross misconduct."* As some incidences of gross misconduct, such as being caught stealing, may warrant summary dismissal, this is simply unrealistic. This will be subject to clarification by the EAT.

1.3.9. Does the employee still have a right of appeal?

Where an employee feels that the disciplinary action taken against them was either wrong, or unjustified, they can still appeal against the decision. The Code says that employees should state the grounds of any such appeal in writing. Once made, an appeal should be dealt with impartially and, ideally, by a manager who hasn't had any prior involvement in the matter.

Appeals should be heard without unreasonable delay and, wherever possible, at a mutually agreed time and place. As before, there's a statutory right to be accompanied at appeal hearings. Once an appeal has been heard, you should inform the employee of the outcome as soon as possible, in writing.

EMPLOYER TIP

If you do dismiss, write to the employee setting out the reasons for your decision. Remind them there's a right of appeal and, to avoid uncertainty, set out the deadline of when this must be made by.

Download Zone

For a **Dismissal with Notice Letter (Misconduct)** and a **Notice of Disciplinary Appeal Hearing**, visit **http://books.indicator.co.uk**. You'll find the access code on page 2 of this book.

1.3.10. What if the employee has committed a criminal offence?

If an employee is charged with, or convicted of, a criminal offence, this won't necessarily be enough for you to take disciplinary action. Instead, you'll need to consider what impact this will have on the employee's suitability to continue in the job, as well as their future working relationships, e.g. with you as the employer, colleagues and customers.

KEY POINTS

In disciplinary matters the Code requires you to:

- initially attempt to resolve the problem informally
- establish the facts
- notify the employee of the evidence against them
- hold a meeting
- allow the employee to bring a companion to the meeting
- decide on appropriate action and notify the employee of this in writing
- allow the employee a right of appeal.

If you don't follow the Code:

- there won't be any automatic finding of unfair dismissal
- a dismissal may still be unfair if you fail to follow a fair procedure
- a tribunal could increase any award by up to 25% if your failure to follow a fair procedure is unreasonable.

1.4. GRIEVANCES - THE CODE

1.4.1. How do we handle a grievance?

The Code emphasises that, wherever possible, grievances should be dealt with informally. If this isn't possible, an employee should raise a complaint formally in writing setting out details of their grievance. Although the phrase "should" is used, there's actually no longer any legal obligation on an employee to do this before bringing a tribunal claim.

EMPLOYER TIP

Don't waste time trying to identify whether an employee is raising a formal grievance or just has a grumble. Unless they've specifically put it in a written grievance, you can safely ignore their complaint.

Download Zone

For a **Grievance Procedure**, visit **http://books.indicator.co.uk**. You'll find the access code on page 2 of this book.

1.4.2. Do we need to arrange a meeting?

When an employee tells you they have a grievance, you need to arrange a formal meeting to discuss it, which should be done without "unreasonable delay". No mention is made of what's considered reasonable, but within five days should suffice (allowing for annual leave or unplanned absences). The parties are expected to make every effort to attend the meeting and the employee raising the grievance should be allowed to explain it and how they think it should be resolved.

EMPLOYER TIP

If, following this meeting, further investigations need to be undertaken, err on the side of caution. Adjourn the meeting so that they can take place.

1.4.3. Does the employee have the right to be accompanied?

There's a statutory right to be accompanied by a companion to a grievance meeting but only where it's being held to deal with a complaint about a duty owed by the employer. Examples of this are where terms of a contract aren't being honoured, or there's a breach of relevant legislation, such as health and safety. Again, tribunal cases will be needed to clarify how far this right extends. As with disciplinary matters, the chosen companion may be a colleague, trade union representative or an official employed by a trade union (certified by their union as being competent).

The companion may also address the hearing, and sum up the case, respond on their behalf to any views expressed at the meeting and to confer with them but they don't have the right to answer questions on the employee's behalf or address the hearing if the employee doesn't want them to.

1.4.4. Are there any restrictions on this right?

The employee must make a *"reasonable request"* to be accompanied - what will be considered reasonable will depend on the circumstances of each case. As with disciplinary hearings, it wouldn't normally be deemed reasonable for a worker to insist on being accompanied by someone whose presence would prejudice the hearing, such as a main witness.

1.4.5. What should we do after the meeting?

After the meeting, decide if you're going to take any action, and if so, what it will be. Irrespective of what decision is reached, you'll need to write to the employee and let them know what (if anything) will be done to resolve the grievance. This letter should also inform them that they can appeal if they're unhappy with the outcome.

1.4.6. What happens if the employee appeals?

They must do this in writing stating the grounds of their appeal. Again, it should be done without *"unreasonable delay"*. Once you've received these grounds, you're also obliged to hear the appeal without unreasonable delay. An appeal hearing should be at a time and place notified to the employee in advance. It should be dealt with impartially and, ideally, heard by a person in authority with no previous involvement, e.g. a manager from a different department or another company director. There's a right to be accompanied to an appeal hearing and the outcome should be communicated to the employee in writing in a timely manner.

1.4.7. What happens if an employee raises a grievance during the disciplinary process?

If, once the disciplinary process has started, an employee raises a grievance, the process can be suspended temporarily so that the employer can deal with it. However, where the two are related, the Code states that it may be more appropriate to deal with them together.

1.4.8. What about grievances raised by a trade union representative?

The Code doesn't apply to any grievances raised by a trade union representative on behalf of two or more employees. These grievances should be handled in accordance with any collective grievance process.

KEY POINTS

For grievances, the Code stipulates that:

- the employee should (not must) inform the employer that they have a grievance
- wherever possible, it should be dealt with informally
- if this isn't possible, then a formal meeting should be held
- where it relates to a complaint about a duty owed by the employer, there's a statutory right to be accompanied to the meeting
- you must decide on the appropriate action and notify the employee of your decision in writing
- there must be a right of appeal
- where a grievance is related to a disciplinary matter that the two can be dealt with together.

If you don't follow the Code:

- a tribunal could increase any award by up to 25% if your failure to follow a fair procedure is unreasonable.

1.5. THE SUPPLEMENTARY ACAS GUIDANCE

1.5.1. Is there any other guidance we should follow?

Supplementary guidance has also been produced by ACAS, which complements the voluntary Code. It gives advice to employers on the expected standards of good practice when dealing with disciplinary matters and grievances. It includes excerpts from the Code and gives information on what steps you can take to comply. In practice, much of its content says nothing new, but it refers to practices that have become established over the last few years.

1.5.2. What is its legal status?

Unlike the new Code, **tribunals are not required to consider the guidance**. The only areas which must be taken into account, are the excerpts from the Code that have been reproduced within it.

1.5.3. What are its main points?

Not only does it contain advice on what's been accepted as good practice for the last few years, but where new points are introduced it attempts to clarify uncertainty caused by new wording used in the Code.

1.5.4. What could happen if we don't follow it?

There's no legal requirement for you to follow the guidance. Equally, there's no duty on a tribunal to consider it when deciding on the outcome of a particular case. It remains to be seen how tribunals will apply it to decisions, even on an informal basis. But it's almost certain they will consider it in order to help them identify whether an employer has followed a fair procedure. So, in our view you should follow its recommendations.

Employer tip

Over time, and as case law develops following the implementation of the new Code, some of the points contained in the supplementary ACAS guidance could acquire legal status.

1.6. DISCIPLINARY MATTERS - THE GUIDANCE

1.6.1. What does the guidance say about formality?

The guidance follows the theme that workplace disputes should, wherever possible, be resolved informally. It states that minor misconduct and/or unsatisfactory performance are the best issues to be dealt with in this way. Like the Code, emphasis is placed on the importance of ensuring that employees understand: **(1)** exactly what they must do in the event disciplinary procedures are brought against them; **(2)** how conduct or performance will be reviewed; and **(3)** over what time period this will happen. This is important as performance issues is an area where many employers come unstuck, purely because they fail to ensure an employee understands exactly what standards they're expected to achieve and maintain.

If, during this informal discussion, it becomes obvious that the matter is more serious, the guidance recommends the meeting should end. In this situation, advise the employee that they will face formal disciplinary procedures. At this point, the guidance also makes reference to independent mediators and suggests they may provide a useful mechanism to resolve the dispute.

Employer tip

Set out any performance issues in writing. Consider whether training or coaching would help the employee improve. This will help to protect your position as you will have laid the foundations of an audit trail should disciplinary proceedings become necessary.

Download Zone

For a **Capability Procedure**, visit **http://books.indicator.co.uk**. You'll find the access code on page 2 of this book.

1

Disciplinary and grievance procedures

1.6.2. What does the guidance say about procedures?

Whilst the Code emphasises the need for procedures to be in writing, specific and clear, the guidance focuses on how this can be achieved. One point that may be overlooked by employers is the benefit of having set standards for conduct and performance. Not only will your workforce know what's expected of them, but you'll be able to act fairly and consistently. Wherever possible, they should apply equally across your business to all levels of staff and be non-discriminatory. The guidance recommends that rules and procedures be developed in conjunction with staff (or their representatives). It's important that employees are made aware of them and know how they can be accessed, e.g. via the staff handbook or Intranet. They can cover issues such as timekeeping, sickness absence, health and safety, use of your business's facilities, discrimination, bullying and harassment, personal appearance and any type of behaviour that will count as misconduct. For smaller businesses, it will be sufficient to display the information in a prominent place.

Employer tip

You may need to brief some employees individually on these rules, e.g. young workers or those who speak English as a second language.

1.6.3. What will a tribunal expect to see in our procedures?

If you're taken to tribunal, your procedures will be closely scrutinised for evidence of best practice. Therefore, it's worth reviewing your existing ones to ensure that they're broadly in line with the stance taken in the revised guidance and that they follow the key theme of fairness. So, check that they: **(1)** provide for matters to be dealt with speedily; **(2)** allow for confidentiality; **(3)** inform employees what disciplinary action might be taken; **(4)** state who is authorised to take it; **(5)** provide that there's no dismissal for a first disciplinary incident (except for gross misconduct); **(6)** require that the matter is fully investigated before taking any disciplinary action; **(7)** state that any period of suspension is brief and is never used as a sanction prior to a disciplinary meeting and decision; **(8)** will keep the employee informed of progress; and **(9)** state that if the facts are disputed, a penalty will not be imposed unless there's a reasonably held belief that the employee committed the act being investigated.

1.6.4. What records does the guidance say we should keep?

There's no getting away from the need to keep good records. The guidance recommends that along with obvious details, such as the nature of a complaint, evidence against the employee and details of any defence raised, records should include the reasons for any action taken. There should also be a detailed note of the outcome of any appeal, as well as details of any grievance raised during the disciplinary process.

1.6.5. How does the guidance say we should investigate a disciplinary matter?

Particular emphasis is placed on conducting investigations in a fair and reasonable manner. As a general rule, the more serious an allegation, the more thorough the subsequent investigation needs to be. Whilst the employee has no statutory right to have a companion present at an investigatory meeting, do give them advance warning of it and time to prepare.

EMPLOYER TIP

If you need to suspend an employee, make it clear that this isn't an assumption of guilt and neither is it a disciplinary sanction.

1.6.6. How does the guidance suggest how we should prepare for a disciplinary hearing?

The guidance offers assistance on obvious issues as well as how to deal with some of the more tricky problems. For example, if an employee's companion can't attend your chosen hearing date, it suggests that you offer a reasonable alternative within five days of your date. Other points cover witnesses, particularly how to deal with those who wish to remain anonymous.

If you find yourself in this position, the guidance stresses the need to seek corroborative evidence and to check that the witness's motives are genuine. Equally, if there's a witness from outside your company who's unwilling, or unable, to attend the meeting, it's normally acceptable to obtain a written statement from them.

EMPLOYER TIP

Try to arrange for someone who isn't involved in the case to be at the meeting to take notes. Ideally, they should be acceptable to both parties.

1.6.7. What does the guidance say about failure to attend a disciplinary hearing?

If you believe that the reason(s) for repeated non-attendance isn't genuine, you're advised to take the following factors into consideration: **(1)** any existing rules that you have for dealing with non-attendance; **(2)** the seriousness of the disciplinary offence; **(3)** the employee's disciplinary record (including current warnings); **(4)** general work record, including work experience, position and length of service; **(5)** medical opinion on whether the employee is fit enough to attend (if relevant); and **(6)** how similar cases have been dealt with previously.

Employer tip

If you do decide to proceed without the employee being present, inform them of this in writing. In that letter, also outline the attempts you've made to rearrange the hearing.

1.6.8. Is there any guidance on how to conduct the hearing?

There's some detail as to how a disciplinary hearing should be conducted. Again, much of this is established good practice, such as introducing the parties and explaining how the hearing will progress. However, there are several points to keep in mind. You should:

- state what the issue is and outline the case by going through the evidence, ensuring that the employee can see and question any witness statements
- allow the employee the opportunity to state their case and answer the allegations
- establish whether the employee accepts that they may have done something wrong
- proceed on written evidence if a witness can't attend and their verbal evidence isn't essential; if it is, postpone the hearing to a later date
- adjourn a hearing to investigate any new facts that emerge
- always adjourn before deciding whether a disciplinary penalty is appropriate.

1.6.9. What does the guidance say about specific problems?

If an employee makes an allegation of bias or discrimination, you're advised to stop the hearing and suspend the disciplinary procedures until they can be investigated.

The same advice applies where a grievance is raised over any evidence that may have been withheld, or if the individual conducting the meeting has an alleged conflict of interest.

Employer tip

If an employee becomes upset, allow a short adjournment so that they can regain their composure, but don't allow it to derail or unnecessarily interrupt the process.

1.6.10. What does the guidance say about the right to be accompanied?

Informal discussions or investigatory meetings don't trigger the right to be accompanied. But where the right does apply, e.g. in disciplinary hearings and appeals, a request doesn't have to be in writing. If you attempt to deny a worker this right, or fail to re-arrange the hearing to allow them to be accompanied, a tribunal may order compensation of up to two weeks' pay (should a complaint be brought).

Employer tip

It remains the case that you should give a chosen companion employed by you a reasonable amount of paid time off to: **(1)** attend the hearing; **(2)** consider the case; and **(3**) confer with the employee.

1.6.11. What does the guidance say we should consider after the disciplinary hearing?

Particular importance is placed on being able to show that a range of factors have been considered when deciding whether any disciplinary action should be taken. Ensure that you're not unfairly singling out an employee and that there aren't any special circumstances that might justify altering the penalty, such as health or domestic problems.

1.6.12. What does the guidance say about disciplinary penalties?

With unsatisfactory performance, the guidance refers to an *"improvement note"*, which is equivalent to a first written warning. This should state that any failure to improve to the required standard in the given timeframe might lead to a final written warning and ultimately dismissal. This should also include details of any support that will be provided to assist the employee, e.g. training.

A copy of the note should be kept and used as the basis for monitoring performance over a specific period, e.g. six months.

Download Zone

For a **Warning of Poor Performance**, visit **http://books.indicator.co.uk**. You'll find the access code on page 2 of this book.

With misconduct, the first written warning should be along similar lines. However, a record of the warning should be kept, but the warning itself should be disregarded for disciplinary purposes after a set period, e.g. six months. If the employee has a current warning, then further problems may justify a final written warning. If so, it can remain current for up to twelve months. You should also include a statement that further misconduct or poor performance may lead to dismissal.

Finally, the guidance clears up some ambiguous wording in the Code as it confirms that, in some cases, dismissal without notice is inevitable, e.g. gross misconduct.

1.6.13. What does the guidance say about the appeals procedure?

The guidance recommends that your appeals procedure should:

- specify a time-limit for lodging an appeal, e.g. five working days
- allow for appeals to be dealt with quickly, particularly those involving dismissal or suspension
- set out the right to be accompanied at any appeal hearing
- state what action may be taken by those hearing the appeal
- allow the employee (or companion) to comment on any new evidence that arises during the appeal before any final decision is made
- provide that the appeal is heard by someone different to the person who took the disciplinary decision; it's important that they are impartial.

1.6.14. What else does the guidance say about appeal hearings?

During any appeal hearing, it's vital that the process is seen to be impartial. With this in mind, the guidance emphasises the need to recognise that changing a previous decision during an appeal won't undermine authority. Instead, it shows that the appeal process is working properly.

Employer tip

If an earlier decision wasn't sound, consider whether your rules need to be clarified or if those involved need further training on how to deal with disciplinary matters.

KEY POINTS

In disciplinary matters, the ACAS supplementary guidance recommends that you:

- ensure the employee knows exactly how they're expected to improve and how their conduct or performance will be reviewed
- confirm in writing what has been discussed during any informal meeting
- set standards for conduct and performance, introduced following consultation with staff and/or their representatives
- have procedures that outline what type of behaviour will qualify as summary dismissal
- have procedures that state what level of management is authorised to take disciplinary action, such as suspension and/or dismissal
- allow a reasonable alternative date for a meeting if an employee's chosen companion can't attend, to take place within five days of the original date
- consider a range of factors including health or domestic problems that may justify a less severe penalty when deciding on the disciplinary penalty
- issue an "improvement note" (equal to a first written warning) where poor performance is the issue.

If you don't follow the guidance:

- you won't be penalised, as there's no legal requirement for you to follow it.

1.7. GRIEVANCES - THE GUIDANCE

1.7.1. How can the guidance help us to develop rules and procedures?

One point made by the guidance concerns the naming of an individual who can be approached if the employee's grievance is against their direct manager. Luckily, it's been recognised that this may not be possible in a small business. Where this happens, it's acceptable to include a statement that the grievance will still be treated fairly and objectively, even where the direct manager may be the cause.

EMPLOYER TIP

Your procedure should also cover third party grievances, e.g. those concerning client/supplier relationships. This type of claim is growing, particularly those relating to discrimination and harassment. A timely way of resolving such problems will only be to your advantage.

1.7.2. What does the guidance say about the right to be accompanied?

The guidance clarifies where there is a right to be accompanied to a grievance hearing. It applies where the complaint concerns a duty owed an employer that's based on legislation or other common law right, such as breach of contract. So, being rejected for a pay rise won't qualify unless the right to that increase is provided for in the contract of employment. But if the grievance relates to equal pay (statutory right), then the right to be accompanied is triggered. In practice, however, it may actually be easier to automatically allow an employee to be accompanied to a formal grievance hearing. Doing otherwise could mean you waste time in trying to identify whether the grievance actually qualifies.

Employer tip

You're entitled to be informed of a proposed companion's identity in advance of the meeting. If they're an official of a trade union not recognised in your workplace, contact them before the meeting to confirm their identity.

1.7.3. What guidance is offered about grievance meetings?

In order to allow consistency of treatment, it's suggested that the individual conducting the grievance hearing identifies whether or not similar issues have been raised previously and, if so, how they were resolved. This will help avoid allegations of discrimination. Likewise, if the individual dealing with the grievance feels unable to make a decision at the time, it's both acceptable and encouraged that you take time to consider it.

1.7.4. Does the guidance give any other recommendations?

It's recommended that if you choose not to uphold an employee's grievance, you fully set out the reason(s) why you have reached this decision. However, should you decide to uphold it, don't underestimate the effect that this could have on other staff. So be prepared to explain your reasoning if the outcome proves unpopular. Also, if a grievance highlights any issues surrounding policies, procedures or conduct, it should be addressed as soon as possible. Finally, you should monitor and review any action taken to ensure that it effectively deals with the grievance.

Key points

For grievances, the new guidance recommends that you:

- ideally name an alternative manager who can be approached should the grievance be about an employee's direct manager
- have procedures that cover third party grievances, e.g. those against and by customers and suppliers
- allow a worker to be accompanied for all types of grievance; not just those where the complaint concerns a legal duty owed by the employer
- always deal with grievances consistently and in a timely manner
- always set out in writing any reasons for not upholding a grievance
- monitor any action taken to ensure that it effectively deals with the grievance.

If you don't follow the guidance:

- you won't be penalised, as there's no legal requirement for you to follow it.

CHAPTER 2

Mediation and the new ACAS Code of Practice

2.1. MEDIATION: AN OVERVIEW

2.1.1. What is mediation?

Mediation is an informal and confidential process in which an impartial third party mediator assists the parties involved in a dispute to try to reach a mutually agreeable and workable solution. It is undertaken with the intention of preserving the parties' relationship and to allow them to continue working with each other. During the process each side has the right to speak openly and honestly about what has caused the disagreement, the impact it has had on them and how they think it can best be resolved. It is entirely voluntary and can take place only if all those involved agree to it. Following a successful mediation the parties' agreement should be put in writing and this can be referred to later if necessary.

2.1.2. What is its relationship to the ACAS Code of Practice?

When the ACAS Code of Practice on Disciplinary and Grievance Procedures (the Code) came into force on April 6 2009 it abolished the statutory procedures that employers had been forced to use. The Code now sets out guidelines that both employers and employees should follow in these situations, and for the very first time they are encouraged to use mediation to try to resolve workplace disputes. This is because, on average, a tribunal claim will cost an employer £9,000 to defend - and that's before any compensation is added, which averages £8,000! Mediation, which can be conducted in-house at very short notice, is viewed as both a cost-effective and time-efficient way to settle disputes, thus avoiding expensive and time-consuming tribunal claims.

2.1.3. Is mediation compulsory?

Although some legal experts recommended that mediation should have been made compulsory, the government didn't go that far. In fact, it has fallen considerably short of giving it any element of compulsion. So, as the law currently stands, a tribunal can't formally penalise the parties for not trying mediation. But it does have the power to reduce or increase an award where one of the parties has acted unreasonably.

Note. Although voluntary in itself, tribunals will take the Code into account when considering a claim and whether the parties have followed its recommendations. Where it feels that they have unreasonably failed to do so, it has the power to adjust compensation by up to 25%. For example, if an employee blatantly refuses to take part in the process and later brings a successful claim, they could see any award slashed by a quarter.

2.1.4. What's the mediator's role in the process?

The mediator should:

- facilitate the meeting
- help the parties identify the issues that are important to them
- remain independent at all times
- steer the discussions towards an agreeable resolution; and
- allow the parties to remain in control of the final outcome.

In other words, they try to bring the parties together by defining the issues and breaking down any communication barriers that have developed. Whilst their role isn't to apportion blame or to decide the outcome, a mediator will often seek concessions from both sides in order to move the process forward.

2.1.5. What's the legal status of mediation?

Mediation isn't a legal process in itself. Nonetheless, it can be used alongside legal proceedings. For example, if tribunal or court proceedings have already been started, an application to have them postponed can be made. Alternatively, a mediator can ask the parties to agree not to launch any legal action whilst the process is underway. However, where the parties settle a dispute through mediation, it will become legally binding when the terms are put into a formal agreement and signed by both parties. The mediator doesn't sign this agreement. At this point, any formal legal proceedings that have already been started must be stopped.

But if mediation fails, all the discussions that took place during it, i.e. those held under the mediator's guidance, are subject to the "without prejudice" rule. This means that they must remain confidential and what was discussed during the process cannot be divulged to a tribunal or court. However, the very fact that mediation took place (even though it wasn't successful) can be disclosed.

Employer tip

If mediation has broken down through no fault of your own, don't be afraid of drawing this to the tribunal's attention. It will be advantageous.

Note. As mediation is a confidential process, the employee can't raise any matters that were discussed in mediation in any subsequent tribunal proceedings. These are out of bounds.

2.1.6. How much money can mediation save us?

It's estimated that employers face total costs of around £17,000 defending a successful tribunal claim, i.e. legal costs and compensation. But a day's mediation will typically cost around a few hundred pounds, less if the process is undertaken in-house.

2.1.7. Are there any other advantages for us?

In addition to saving you money, mediation can help your business in other ways. For example:

- **Time saving.** Even with those cases that wouldn't go to tribunal, early intervention via mediation has the potential to save considerable management time later on.
- **Flexibility.** The process is highly flexible and can be continually adapted to fit the needs of the parties. As a result, ACAS has found it to be successful in around 70-80% of cases.
- **Control.** As mediation is voluntary, both you and the employee stay in control of what happens. In other words, there isn't a resolution unless both sides agree it. This is unlike a tribunal decision which is imposed on the parties and often penalises the employer.
- **Informality.** You don't need to have easy access to dedicated human resources professionals or specialist employment law expertise to undertake the process.
- **Tribunal ammunition.** You can also use the fact you attempted it to your advantage if you do have to defend yourself in tribunal.
- **Reputation.** The media love to report the details of tribunal claims and whilst you're probably used to seeing the sizeable awards in the national press, the local press like to do their fair share of reporting too, particularly if a well-known local business is involved. Even if you win the case, there is always a risk that existing and potential clients and employees will see your name. As mediation takes place away from the public's gaze, your business reputation will remain intact.

2.1.8. Are there any disadvantages?

There are a few, but they won't be a problem if you go about things in the right way.

Rogue operators. The first issue to watch out for is the current lack of industry regulation. At present, anyone can set up as a mediator without having any formal training. In fact, as mediation gains more prominence, it's likely that many organisations, or individuals, will see it as a way to make easy money. So, your business could be vulnerable to the "cowboy" element. This comes with an added risk that these rogue operators won't have any professional indemnity cover. But by checking the mediator's background, qualifications and experience you can be sure that they are properly accredited and a professional in their field.

Employees' view. Employees can be suspicious of a process that they believe is being organised and driven by their employer - even if it is with the intention of resolving the matter! Due to the increasingly adversarial nature of employment disputes, some employees may decide to shun mediation, and have their day in court. This may be because they have an unrealistic view of their likelihood of winning a claim and how much it is worth if they do. This belief is often generated by the widespread media focus on very large (but rare) compensatory awards.

EMPLOYER TIP

Since mediation is voluntary, you can't force an employee to participate but you can explain the process to them and how it works. Remind them that if they lose without having given the process a go, the tribunal can knock up to 25% off any award - assuming they get one in the first place!

Restricted to current employees. Finally, mediation relies on the employee still being employed. Depending on the nature of a dispute, this may not always be the case. For example, if the employee has already resigned, then you can't use it. If such an employee raises a dispute, then you will have to resolve it another way, e.g. compromise agreement.

2.1.9. Is mediation suitable for smaller businesses?

Yes. It's ideal for the type of problems that small businesses tend to experience, such as disciplinary issues and relationship breakdowns. These can escalate unnecessarily as there's unlikely to be a dedicated department to deal with conflict management. With the further benefit of it being a relatively cheap option, particularly where in-house mediators are used, it's certainly recommended for smaller companies.

Key points

Mediation is:

- a voluntary process
- used where discussions between an employer and employee have broken down
- a cost-effective way to avoid a tribunal claim and damage to your reputation.

A mediator:

- is a neutral third party who assists the parties in reaching a settlement
- identifies the issues and steers the discussions
- remains impartial throughout the process.

Mediation is being promoted because it:

- allows the parties and not the mediator to remain in control of the outcome
- is much cheaper and far less time consuming than defending a tribunal claim
- is flexible and can be tailored to suit the needs of each case
- is particularly suited to small businesses that lack in-house expertise in employment law and conflict management
- is ideal for resolving disciplinary issues and breakdowns in working relationships.

Mediation has some disadvantages for the unwary, namely that:

- it's not regulated as an industry, so anyone can call themselves a mediator
- employees may be suspicious of a process that they see as being employer-led
- by thinking they might miss out on a payout, some employees may want their day in court
- it can't be used if an employee is no longer working for you.

2.2. MEDIATION IN THE WORKPLACE

2.2.1. What types of dispute can be resolved via mediation?

There's a wide range of employment disputes that are suitable for mediation. At one end of the spectrum lie those of a more informal nature that focus on workplace relationships, such as personality clashes and minor gripes. At the other end are those which could clearly be headed for tribunal (or county or High Court) if there's no early intervention. These could include grievances alleging some form of discrimination, e.g. sex or age, or where the outcome could justify dismissal, e.g. over poor performance. In the middle, are standard disciplinary issues where a more sympathetic approach could prompt a better response than immediate formal disciplinary proceedings. For example, if an employee is persistently late, or has a high rate of one-day sickness absence, you may be able to resolve the problem via mediation rather than making it a capability or poor performance issue.

Research shows that in many cases, where an employer proceeds straight to a formal hearing, the employee concerned will often go off sick with stress in order to derail proceedings. The added problem here is that they could land you with a claim for personal injury. But by using a neutral third party mediator you can explore a wider range of options that will be binding once there is a formal agreement.

2.2.2. Are any disputes not suited to mediation?

Yes, there are some, mainly those where the subject matter offers little, if any, room to manoeuvre and negotiate. Common examples include:

- **Employment contracts.** This could include disputes over annual leave allowance, pension entitlement and the operation of any bonus schemes.
- **Company policies.** The same applies to complaints over your policies, such as an Internet use policy or redundancy selection criteria.
- **Statutory compliance.** Where challenges are made to policies that exist as a result of having to comply with statutory requirements, e.g. financial reporting requirements, environmental and health and safety matters.
- **Gross misconduct.** If the employee has committed an act of gross misconduct, e.g. theft, and your only option is to dismiss them.
- **Criminal activities.** Where criminal activity is involved, such as fraud or violence.

Should an employee wish to challenge these issues, they must do so in the correct way - mediation is not the right forum in which to air them.

2.2.3. Must we tell employees about the possibility of mediation?

As mediation isn't compulsory you're not compelled to inform employees of its existence. Nevertheless, it's in your interest to do so as it can help you avoid the cost and time involved in preparing for, and defending, a tribunal claim. The easiest way to do this is with a mediation policy.

Download Zone

For a **Mediation Policy** and **Letter Inviting Employee to Mediation**, visit **http://books.indicator.co.uk**. You'll find the access code on page 2 of this book.

2.2.4. When can we start mediation?

There's no defined point as to when it should start but ACAS says that where a conflict arises, mediation should be used to "nip it in the bud". This means it should come into play if those involved in the disagreement, e.g. two co-workers, can't resolve it between themselves. So it should be considered when the parties become entrenched and the conflict would only continue or otherwise lead to you having to instigate your formal grievance or disciplinary procedures if you don't act.

2.2.5. Can we select a mediator from within our business?

Yes, but you might not want to use an in-house mediator in all cases. They are more suitable for disputes involving disagreements between co-workers, or an employee and their line manager, or for allegations of bullying, favouritism and being overlooked for promotions. In other words, the type of dispute that isn't likely, at least for the foreseeable future, to lead to the employee resigning and/or bringing a claim.

Employer tip

If you use an internal mediator, they must have the authority to settle the dispute. Ideally, they should be more senior than the parties involved.

2.2.6. When should we use an external mediator?

Sometimes it will be more effective to resolve disputes using an accredited external mediator. This is advisable where you can't identify someone from within your organisation who is definitely impartial (and this is agreed by both sides).

Also, disputes that are moving rapidly towards either tribunal or court can benefit from specialist intervention; for example, over the termination of an employment contract or a high value contractual claim, e.g. for unpaid bonuses. In these cases, the discussions may be highly sensitive and best facilitated by an external mediator. Also, in complicated disputes, the drafting of any binding agreement will need to be done with a certain amount of expertise and precision. Many professional mediators are either qualified lawyers or hold other qualifications which will protect your business.

Employer tip

Depending on your likely need for an external mediator, consider entering into an agreement with a single mediator to provide services on an ad hoc basis - this could be cheaper.

Download Zone

For a **Letter Requesting Information From an External Mediator**, visit **http://books.indicator.co.uk**. You'll find the access code on page 2 of this book.

2.2.7. How much can we expect to pay?

There's no set rate for mediators. However, many will ask for a one-off fee to prepare for the session and the first few hours' work. They will then charge on an hourly basis if it goes over this estimate. Alternatively, they may charge an hourly rate from the start. Either way, when asking for an estimate, be realistic about the work involved - if there's a large amount of paperwork or you think the parties will have a great deal to speak about, say so. This will avoid nasty surprises for them and a bigger bill for you!

Employer tip

If using an external mediator for the first time, don't hesitate in asking for a discount. If they want to secure your business in a highly competitive field, they should be prepared to do this.

2.2.8. How can we persuade a reluctant employee to take part in mediation?

You will generally have two main problems to overcome. The first is that they may be suspicious of a process that's organised by their employer. The second is that they may have an unrealistic view of the merits and potential value of their claim, largely brought about by the false impressions created by the media.

To get around this you will first need to demonstrate why your process will be impartial. If the employee simply won't agree to your choice of internal mediator, your best option is to use an external mediator. If you do, emphasise the fact that this individual will be unknown to the business and truly independent.

Also, make it clear that the employee will have plenty of opportunity to meet with the mediator during the day's session without you being present. Remind them that full confidentiality applies to the process.

As for wanting to have their day in court, you can do two things. Firstly, you can point out that the average compensation payout is only £8,000, which is considerably less than the six-figure payouts often quoted in the papers. Also, tell them that only 7% of employees who take their employer to a tribunal remain in their jobs afterwards, and those who don't are usually refused a reference.

2.2.9. Why is confidentiality so important?

Some of the content of the mediator's discussions is likely to include very personal information and/or it may reveal too much about one party's bargaining position before they want the other side to know about it. For this reason, after each private meeting, the mediator (be it an internal or external one) must always ask each party what they can tell the other side after the discussion and what they must keep confidential.

2.2.10. What if there's a problem after mediation?

In a minority of cases, the parties may experience further difficulties following mediation. But irrespective of whether or not these difficulties could lead to a tribunal claim, the parties are likely to want the mediator to give evidence as to what was said during the mediation.

However, this won't be possible because the purpose of mediation is to allow a full and frank discussion to take place. So, details of the session must remain confidential afterwards and cannot be used in future proceedings. In other words, the mediation process is subject to the "without prejudice" rule. If an external mediator is involved, their terms will usually state that they're unable to have any involvement in a future tribunal claim - for either side.

Note. Any written notes from a mediation session (apart from any agreement that has been drafted) should be destroyed immediately after the matter has been concluded.

Employer tip

Although it may seem pointless, suggest that the parties consider a further attempt at mediation in order to resolve the new dispute. There's nothing to stop you from using the same mediator. It may even be more cost effective as you won't have to go over old ground.

Key points

Disputes that are suitable for mediation include:

- relationship breakdowns
- dignity at work issues
- grievances
- conduct and capability issues
- those involving allegations of discrimination
- where dismissal could arise if there was no intervention.

Mediation isn't appropriate where the dispute involves:

- disagreements over employment contracts or company policy
- challenges to policies that exist for the purpose of statutory compliance
- instances of gross misconduct where the only option is dismissal, e.g. for theft
- a complaint raised by an ex-employee.

Other key points to bear in mind:

- mediation should be used at the point where the parties have become entrenched
- if you use an internal mediator, they must have the authority to settle the dispute
- relationship breakdowns are best suited to internal mediation
- external mediators should be used for disputes that could end up in court
- mediators can't give evidence about what was said during mediation.

2.3. CHOOSING AN INTERNAL MEDIATOR

2.3.1. What type of person makes a good mediator?

The wrong choice of mediator could easily lead to accusations of bias and worsen relations between you and the other side. So, with this in mind, only pursue the internal mediation route if you can identify one or more individuals with the right personal attributes.

This will be someone who:

- the parties respect
- is unbiased and impartial, i.e. they've had no prior involvement in any capacity
- can be flexible
- is friendly; and
- is of a sufficiently senior level.

This final point is important as an internal mediator needs to be seen to have authority by the parties.

2.3.2. What personal skills do they need?

Your chosen candidate will need a combination of the following:

- **Listening skills.** This doesn't just refer to picking up on what is actually said by the parties but an ability to be able to read between the lines. From this they can steer the process more effectively and encourage the parties to express views they might otherwise be reluctant to air.
- **Empathy.** A good mediator will need to be able to show empathy with both sides and demonstrate that they understand why they feel as they do (even if they dislike one or both parties). If the parties feel uncomfortable with a mediator, the process will stand little chance of success.
- **Patience.** Mediation can be a frustrating process, particularly if one or both parties become entrenched in their views and won't budge. Therefore, patience and the ability to be able to move the parties forward is essential.
- **Negotiation skills.** Apart from the risk of deadlock, one or both of the parties may believe that mediation isn't working and won't see any point in continuing. This is where the ability to negotiate and steer both sides through a stalemate will come to the fore.
- **Creativity and problem-solving skills.** As deadlock between the parties is quite common, a good mediator will be able to find new ways of looking at problems and do so in a way that engages both sides.

2.3.3. Why must they be impartial?

If the mediator shows bias, or favouritism, in some way, even unintentionally, it's likely to derail the process very quickly.

Note. Clear impartiality means that there can be no accusation that one side didn't have an equal say in the process.

2.3.4. Do they need any formal training?

There's no legal requirement for an internal mediator to have received any formal training. However, an untrained mediator could have an adverse impact on a dispute, so we would advise you to at least consider basic training, particularly if you think that you're likely to make fairly frequent use of mediation.

One provider that you shouldn't go wrong with is ACAS (**http://www.acas.org.uk**). They offer several courses ranging from a half-day "Introduction to Mediation" through to a five-day accredited "Certificate in Internal Mediation".

KEY POINTS

An ideal candidate for an internal mediator is someone who is:

- respected by the parties
- seen to be unbiased and impartial
- flexible
- friendly
- of a sufficiently senior level.

A mediator needs:

- good listening skills and an ability to read between the lines
- the ability to show empathy with both parties
- patience, as mediation can be frustrating if one or both sides won't budge
- good negotiation skills to steer the parties through a deadlock
- creativity and problem-solving attributes
- to remain impartial at all times
- formal training ranging from half a day to five days depending on your needs.

2.4. SELECTING EXTERNAL MEDIATORS

2.4.1. How do we find a suitable mediator?

If you wish to bring in an external mediator to help resolve the dispute, you need to know how to avoid the cowboys that are likely to enter the market on the back of the recommendations of the Code. Your best bet is to use a mediator who has been accredited by the Civil Mediation Council (CMC).

The CMC was formed in 2003 to act as an umbrella body. Apart from requiring certain professional standards of conduct from those wishing to be members, it also sets minimum requirements, e.g. insurance cover and continuing professional development. As this is the closest that you will find to an official body at the current time, we would recommend that you only use an eternal mediator who is a member of the CMC.

Employer tip

You can quickly find out who is a member of the CMC from its website **http://www.civilmediation.org/** or by calling 020 7353 322. It will offer advice on accredited mediators, and will let you know the limit of their experience, expertise and location.

2.4.2. What should we look for?

Be clear at the outset what you're looking for. This is because a number of dispute resolution companies offer arbitration as well as mediation (arbitration is where the parties agree to be bound by the final decision of an independent arbitrator). Mediation also covers a variety of different disputes, including family and commercial matters, such as complex construction disputes. What you need is a mediator who deals in "workplace" mediation.

To give you a head start, the following are websites of long-established and reputable mediation companies that cover this area:

- ADR Group - **http://www.adrgroup.co.uk**
- British Academy of Experts - **http://www.academy-experts.org**
- Centre for Effective Dispute Resolution - **http://www.cedr.co.uk**
- Mediation UK - **http://www.ukmediation.net**

2.4.3. What questions should we ask them?

You should ensure that any mediator you're offered is right for your business. Ask the following questions:

- **What experience do you have?** A newly accredited mediator won't be a problem for more basic disputes, e.g. those involving workplace relationships, but do insist on a more experienced person for complex situations.
- **What training have you undertaken?** Recently qualified mediators should have completed a course of 40 hours' duration. This will include theory and practical work. You also want to know about ongoing training - a certificate that's a number of years old could mean they're not on top of industry developments.
- **What is your success rate?** Whilst they can't disclose client names they can tell how many cases they resolve. As a rough guide, anything over 80% is a good strike rate.

- **Are you a member of any professional bodies?** Although the mediation industry remains unregulated, the Civil Mediation Council acts as a governing body. As over 400 organisations have membership, it's worth checking that your chosen provider is one of them.
- **Do you have insurance?** Always ask for a copy of the mediator's professional indemnity insurance.
- **Can we see some references?** Happy clients will give references - so avoid the mediator who can't produce any!

Download Zone

For a **Letter Requesting Information from an External Mediator**, visit **http://books.indicator.co.uk**. You'll find the access code on page 2 of this book.

2.4.4. When do we pay the mediator?

As a general rule, you will need to pay the mediator in advance of the mediation session for their preparation time and the "agreed hours". Anything that goes over this will be billed separately.

2.4.5. Does the employee share the cost?

No. Unlike commercial mediation (where both sides split the costs equally), you are expected to pay the mediator.

KEY POINTS

When looking for an external mediator:

- contact the Civil Mediation Council (CMC) for details of accredited mediators
- avoid using a mediator that isn't accredited by the CMC as they won't be regulated
- for complex disputes, find out what experience they have
- ask about their success rate in workplace mediations
- use newly accredited mediators for more straightforward disputes
- ask for a copy of the mediator's professional indemnity insurance cover
- ask what mediation training they have received. For those having trained more recently, the industry standard is a course lasting 40 hours.

2.5. THE MEDIATION PROCESS

2.5.1. Why is the room set-up so important?

The mediation process is sufficiently fraught without having to worry about the comfort of the participants. For this reason, environmental and other ambient factors are very important when choosing the location. You should think about the following:

- the area should be quiet and private. Extraneous noise such as fax machines, ringing telephones and busy areas should be avoided
- you will need a meeting room for each party and a larger one for joint sessions
- the rooms should be clutter-free and tidy
- office equipment such as a fax machine, printer and laptop should be accessible
- refreshments such as coffee, tea and water should be readily available
- the basics such as paper, pens, flip chart and marker pens should be provided. Also have a supply of tissues to hand!

EMPLOYER TIP

When setting up the table for the joint session, don't have the parties facing each other on opposite sides of the desk. Instead, use a round table, or if one isn't available, sit the parties at the corners but on the same side of the table.

2.5.2. What are the stages of mediation?

➤ *1. Preparation*

Whilst much of the focus of mediation is what occurs on the day, the need for careful preparation must not be overlooked. How this works in practice will depend on whether an internal or external mediator is conducting the mediation.

If they're external, the mediator will contact the parties by phone prior to the session to establish the basic facts, identify those involved, the history of the dispute and to schedule a date and time for the mediation.

Employer tip

They may also want to speak to someone within your organisation who has responsibility for personnel, in order to: **(1)** obtain your policies relating to the subject matter under dispute; **(2)** find out if it's a one-off dispute; and **(3)** if not, how similar disputes have been dealt with previously.

➤ *2. Opening session*

A mediation session always starts with an opening statement from the mediator. Apart from providing important information, they will set out the behaviour that's expected from the parties. With this in mind, the opening statement should include the following information:

- **Introductions.** Ensure that everyone is introduced and that their role in the mediation is made clear. Also check how the parties would like to be addressed, e.g. first names or surnames.
- **Describing mediation.** Explain that mediation is voluntary, non-binding to the point of an agreement and that the discussions are "without prejudice" (briefly explain what this means). Make it clear that full confidentiality applies and that it's down to the parties to find their own solution.
- **Process.** Describe how the mediation process will work. In particular, explain that it will contain both joint and private sessions. Make it clear that you may spend longer with one party than the other, depending on the issues being discussed but that this has no reflection on the outcome.
- **Mediation ground rules**. This is your opportunity to stress the importance of each side allowing the other to speak without interruption. Ask the parties to refrain from swearing and other bad behaviour.
- **Your role.** Make it clear that your role is that of a facilitator. Therefore, you will guide discussions, clarify the issues and act as "Devil's Advocate" by asking difficult questions. Also explain that you're not there as a judge.
- **Confidentiality.** It's important to stress that the discussions held with each party in their private rooms will remain confidential unless the party gives you express permission to divulge certain points to the other side. Remind the parties that tape recorders aren't allowed.
- **Any questions**. Finally, ask the parties if they have any questions before you begin.

After the mediator's opening statement, the complainant (the party instigating the dispute) also makes an opening statement. This sets out their version of events and what they want to see happen. For example, in a relationship breakdown between an employee and their manager, the employee may want nothing more than an apology and an agreement that they will be managed differently (at this stage, many disputes don't involve money, which is why mediation is an attractive form of dispute resolution).

Whilst the complainant is speaking, the other side may wish to make notes, but they should not interrupt. When finished, it is the turn of the other party to make their opening statement. Again, the other side should remain quiet.

EMPLOYER TIP

If you're acting as the mediator, don't make notes during this opening session. Just listen and get a feel for the issues that are emerging.

At this point, you will need to split the parties and introduce them to their separate meeting rooms. Before you do this, decide which party you will speak to first in private.

Convention dictates that you should start with the complainant/aggrieved party. However, if the other side raises a particularly important point in their opening statement, you may meet with them first. This is more unusual, but if you choose to do so explain why this is, e.g. you wish to clarify a point that could have a substantial impact on the mediation.

➤ *3. Exploration of issues*

During the private meetings, be prepared for one or both parties (particularly the employee) to want to unburden themselves. This could include a lot of personal information that doesn't seem relevant to the area(s) under discussion. Whilst it's understandable to want to either hurry them along or stop them, don't.

It's very important that each side feels that they can speak freely. So be patient and say as little as possible, but when you do, never give a personal opinion. Where possible, encourage each side to express their feelings early on in the day. By doing this, both parties can get matters off their chest and hopefully move on towards finding a resolution to the dispute. Don't forget that each party may have considerable emotional investment in their version of events, so allow for this.

You can periodically interject by summarising the information that you have been given. This not only reassures the parties that you are actively listening to them, but also allows you to: **(1)** check your understanding of what you're being told; **(2)** identify recurring themes and key words used; and **(3)** discover underlying issues. This is the time to start making notes about the key points.

At this stage also be aware of the differences between the following:

- **Position.** This refers to how a party to the proceedings believes that it should be resolved. In other words, it's a demand for a particular solution, e.g. *"Joe Bloggs and I cannot work together, so one of us must be moved to a different office".*
- **Interests.** This is a concern which is the motivating force behind the party adopting a particular position, e.g. *"I think that the working environment will greatly improve if Joe Bloggs is moved elsewhere".*
- **Needs.** This is the underlying and often unspoken issue that has pushed the parties into dispute. In this scenario, it's likely to arise from a mutual dislike so the party mediating needs recognition that they are the "wronged" party. In other cases, it will arise out of some other form of conflict, e.g. collapse of a workplace relationship.

After you've had your first private meeting with one party, move to the other private meeting room to meet with the other side. At this stage you should first listen to what the other party (usually the employer) has to say, before divulging information that you have been given by the other side.

Note. Before leaving to meet with the other party, always ask what information may be disclosed and what must remain confidential.

EMPLOYER TIP

Always start with a clean page in your notebook - you don't want to let the other party see your notes.

➤ *4. Negotiation*

After you have met privately with both parties, you will have started to form an opinion about the dispute and the relative merits of each side's argument. Keep your thoughts to yourself at this stage. You should then bring the parties back to the joint meeting room and outline the areas that were discussed; leaving out any information or concessions that you have been told are confidential (at least at this stage). Once you've done this, obtain input from each party, starting with the first one that you met with privately. Whilst doing this, make notes and read them back to the parties. Get confirmation as to their accuracy. Where common ground is emerging, highlight it. This shows that progress is being made.

At this stage, you should note the different negotiation styles that will be deployed by the parties. Whilst you may not be able to do much, if anything, about them, you can at least be aware of what to look for. Once you've identified which ones you're dealing with, you can tailor your response accordingly. They are as follows:

- **Integrative.** From your point of view, this approach is the easiest to deal with. This is where the party's focus is on mutual gain. So they will willingly explore all options including those areas that aren't subject to disagreement. The idea is that there will be two winners emerging from a collaborative style of mediation.
- **Positional.** As its name suggests, those adopting this style tend to highlight the differences between the parties instead of focusing on common ground. To this end, one or both parties will use pressure to try to manoeuvre the other into offering more than they need.
- **Distributive.** This is an adversarial approach based on winning and losing. It sees one party's gain as the other's loss. A party adopting this approach wants the outcome "distributed" as much as possible in their favour.

Once you've got as far as you can in this joint session be prepared to send the parties off to their individual rooms again. But before you do, summarise what you see as the key points and ask the parties to confirm their agreement. Also run through areas of common ground and those that are still disputed or otherwise unresolved. The outcome of this process will shape the next round of private discussions. This process of private sessions followed by a joint session will continue until both sides (ideally) have reached agreement.

EMPLOYER TIP

Don't hesitate in having unscheduled breaks or time on your own, as you are the one setting the schedule.

➤ *5. Closing*

If agreement is reached, it's formalised at the closing joint session. The written Agreement, prepared by the mediator, will need to be signed by both parties.

However, if no agreement has been reached, ask the parties if it's worth extending the mediation. Ideally, this would involve an extension into the evening in order to maintain momentum. But if not, it would mean re-scheduling another shorter session for another day. If an external mediator is being used, they will charge an extra fee for this. If no agreement has been reached and is unlikely to be forthcoming in the future, the closing session should be used to highlight the progress that has been made. It's also the last opportunity that the mediator will have to outline the remaining issues and encourage the parties to make one last attempt at resolving them, possibly before a tribunal claim. You may find that this concentrates the parties' minds sufficiently to seek a settlement. Irrespective of what happens, the parties should be thanked by the mediator for their efforts. Finally, the mediator should destroy their notes, preferably by shredding them on site.

Employer tip

If the mediation goes on "after hours", ensure that you have the telephone number of the managing or financial director who has the authority to agree any financial settlement.

Download Zone

For a **Mediation Checklist**, visit **http://books.indicator.co.uk**. You'll find the access code on page 2 of this book.

2.5.3. Are there any other points we need to remember?

In addition to the points mentioned above, you should also bear the following in mind:

- don't try to solve problems for the parties unless and until they have run out of ideas
- resist the temptation to categorise the issues and force a solution too quickly
- don't create possibilities and solutions that just won't work
- just convey what has been said between the parties; don't exaggerate
- don't get drawn into giving your personal opinion on matters
- finally, remember that whilst you're not in charge of the outcome, you are in charge of the process.

2.5.4. Is mediation legally binding?

Mediation isn't legally binding until the point that an agreement that suits all parties has been reached. This will only happen when all relevant points under discussion are recorded in writing and signed by both parties.

2.5.5. How long should the process take from start to finish?

With a careful approach, many disputes can be resolved in three to four hours, although some may last a whole day.

KEY POINTS

The stages to mediation are:

- preparation
- opening session
- exploration
- negotiation
- closing session.

At the opening session outline the following points:

- ensure that everyone is introduced and that their role is clarified
- explain what mediation is and how the day will work
- set out the ground rules with regards to the parties' behaviour
- describe the role of the mediator
- explain the confidentiality aspect of mediation
- the parties should be asked if they have any questions.

Key points for in-house mediators to remember are:

- don't try to solve problems unless the parties have run out of ideas themselves
- resist the temptation to categorise the issues and force a solution too quickly
- avoid creating possibilities that won't work
- during the private sessions, just convey what one party has said, don't exaggerate
- you are in charge of the mediation process
- never get drawn into giving your personal opinion.

2.6. TROUBLESHOOTING

2.6.1. The employee wants to bring a workplace companion - do we let them?

The choice is yours but their role must be clear. Employees do not have the statutory right to be accompanied in this type of forum, but it may be sensible to allow them to bring a companion who can provide moral support, particularly if they are outnumbered, as it shows you have acted fairly. But do exercise caution in who you allow to be present; after all it's private business you're discussing, so you don't want it becoming public. Therefore, only allow a workplace colleague.

Employer tip

Lawyers and trade union representatives should be kept out of mediation. It's an informal process and whilst there's nothing that prohibits their attendance, they probably won't help matters. They're likely to focus on the legal issues rather than the practicalities.

2.6.2. How do we break a deadlock?

It's quite likely that at some point during mediation, the parties will reach deadlock with neither wishing to move far from their position. This can happen for a number of reasons, such as running out of ideas, tiredness, or a feeling that there are no new ways of looking at the problem.

Should this situation arise, use one, or a combination, of the following tactics in order to break the deadlock:

- be honest and acknowledge that a deadlock exists. Ask the parties to help find a way out of it
- have a break
- remind both sides how both will benefit by resolving the dispute and how far you have already progressed (if applicable)
- recap the issue which is the sticking point. If it's a relatively small one, it might make the parties realise how far they have come and the futility of losing the momentum
- give the parties a reality check by asking them to outline their "best alternative to a negotiated settlement" and "worst alternative to a negotiated settlement". This will help to focus their minds
- As a last resort, give a deadline by which something further must be resolved before you terminate the mediation.

Employer tip

To help avoid unnecessary anger and resentment, try to see that potential conflict is diffused early on in the process.

2.6.3. What's the best way to deal with a nervous employee?

Wherever possible, try to ensure that the parties arrive at slightly different times. The more vulnerable party should be first. In the context of workplace mediation, this will usually be the employee.

Also, depending on the layout of the table during a joint session, seat the more vulnerable party nearest to you. Much research has been carried out into the psychological effects of seating arrangements and it's been found that the further away from the mediator a more vulnerable party is, the worse they feel.

EMPLOYER TIP

Check at the outset whether first names are to be used. If so, make it clear that it applies to the employee and employer representative(s) in order to create a level playing field.

2.6.4. How do we deal with anger?

Depending on the nature of the dispute and how long it's been going on for, you may find that one of the parties (most usually the employee) displays anger and/or aggression. Not only could this derail the mediation, but it could undermine the mediator's authority if it isn't dealt with effectively. Therefore, stay calm and work through the following steps:

Step 1. Vent anger. Allow the angry party to vent their anger before interrupting them (or at least until they visibly start to cool down). This can also help reveal the real issues behind the dispute that may not have been given at the initial joint session. Don't contradict them or undermine their views.

Step 2. Show empathy. Use empathy, rather than sympathy, to diffuse the anger by using phrases such as *"I can see why you feel this way"* or *"I can see your point of view"*. Avoid saying *"calm down"*, which is more likely to inflame the situation.

Step 3. Get back on track. The time to get proceedings back on track is when the angry party starts becoming repetitive. At this point, interject and explain that whilst you're grateful to have had the opportunity to fully understand the situation and the strength of their feelings, due to time constraints you need to move the mediation forward.

Step 4. Summarise the issues. Get the parties to re-focus by using this as another opportunity to summarise the issues. Clarify those that you think are important and will move proceedings forward, and outline those that you feel should be dropped. Getting the parties back on track in this way will also help diffuse any feelings of awkwardness or embarrassment following an angry outburst.

Step 5. Stay neutral. Even if you consider an issue to be irrelevant, the parties may not. So as it's their dispute, deal with the issue without getting drawn into any arguments yourself.

Employer tip

If one of the parties won't calm down, try suspending the mediation session for a short time. If this fails, adjourn the session to another day as it's pointless continuing.

2.6.5. If it all goes wrong can the mediator give evidence on our behalf?

No, this is not possible. But you can tell the tribunal you attempted mediation - just not what was discussed.

Key points

You can break a deadlock by:

- asking the parties to help find a way through it
- taking a break and encouraging the parties to get some fresh air
- reminding the parties of the progress they have made so far
- recapping the issue that is the subject of the deadlock
- asking the parties to outline their best and worst alternative to settling
- giving a deadline by which something further must be resolved before you end the mediation.

Deal with anger by:

- allowing the angry party to express it
- showing empathy to the angry party's point of view
- gently reminding the party concerned that you must move matters forward
- summarising the issues in order to get the parties to re-focus
- always remaining neutral
- adjourning the mediation for a break to allow the parties to cool down.

CHAPTER 3

Avoiding and managing employment tribunal claims

3.1. WHO CAN BRING A TRIBUNAL CLAIM?

3.1.1. When will this situation arise?

Within any workplace disputes can arise. Although employers will try to resolve them quickly and cost-effectively, their chosen approach isn't always successful. In April 2009, following the abolition of statutory disciplinary, dismissal and grievance procedures, ACAS produced a new voluntary Code of Practice on Disciplinary and Grievance Procedures (the Code) that aims to help employers deal with these matters. In addition, and for the first time, it also recommended mediation. This process is undertaken by a neutral third party mediator who tries to identify a workable solution for all the parties.

In many cases, following the Code, or going through mediation, will bring the dispute to a satisfactory conclusion. But sometimes these approaches simply don't work - particularly where you are dealing with a hotheaded employee who wants their "day in court". In this situation, you may be on the receiving end of an employment tribunal claim. Even if it doesn't make it all the way to a hearing, it can be costly and time-consuming.

This chapter will not only take you through the tribunal process, but provide practical and cost-effective advice on how to respond to a claim. It also explains the role of ACAS in the employment tribunal process, the advantages of compromise agreements and how you can best prepare your side of the case for any subsequent hearing.

3.1.2. What claims can a tribunal hear?

More than 100 claims can be brought to the tribunal's attention, but by far the most common are:

- unfair dismissal, including redundancy
- discrimination, including harassment, bullying and victimisation
- breach of contract
- equal pay
- non-payment of wages.

3.1.3. Can anyone bring a tribunal claim?

It's a common misconception that only employees with one year's service can bring a tribunal claim. In reality, it's much more complex than that. Not only will it depend on the individual's employment status, much rests on the type of claim.

Employer tip

In the employment tribunal, the party bringing the case, i.e. the employee, is called the "claimant" and the other party, i.e. the employer, the "respondent".

3.1.4. What is meant by employment status?

For claims such as unfair dismissal or redundancy pay, an individual must be an "employee" who works under a "contract of service". This will probably cover most, if not all, of the people working for you. However, there are some claims that can be started by "workers". These individuals are not employees; they are, for example, temporary workers, or freelance contractors, i.e. they must perform the work personally.

Note. Whilst workers are not employees, all employees are classed as workers.

Employer tip

If an individual can't be classified as either an employee or a worker, they will not have any rights to commence a tribunal claim.

3.1.5. What claims can a worker pursue?

Firstly, they can bring claims under the **Working Time Regulations 1998**, for example if they are denied their entitlement to statutory minimum holiday, or are dismissed because they refused to work more than a 48-hour week. In addition, they can:

- claim discrimination on the grounds of sex, sexual orientation, race, disability, age, religion or belief or sexual orientation
- demand to be paid the National Minimum Wage; and
- claim protection under the **Part Time Workers Regulations 2000** if they are a part-time worker.

Employer tip

It's not uncommon for self-employed people who lose a contract to go to tribunal and attempt to argue that they were, in reality, a worker or an employee - it can be in their financial interests to do so. So make sure that the contracts of these individuals are clear as to what relationship exists between the parties and be careful in the way that you conduct it. For example, subjecting them to your disciplinary and/or sickness absence procedure could allow the tribunal to conclude that they are, in fact, an employee.

3.1.6. Must individuals be employed at the point they start a tribunal claim?

No, not only can they do this after employment has ended, they can attempt to claim discrimination without you even offering them a job or calling them for an interview. In fact, there are individuals out there who make a living from setting up unwary employers in the hope that they will turn them down so they can claim discrimination. A favourite method of doing this is to submit two identical applications. For example, an Asian person seeking to allege race discrimination will send one application in their real name and another in a name which implies that they are non-Asian. If the employer rejects the application submitted in their own name, yet offers an interview to the other "candidate", the individual has everything they need to successfully claim race discrimination. In this situation, there is little, if anything, that the employer can do about it.

There is, however, some good news for employers. The Employment Appeal Tribunal (EAT) recently held in **Keane v Investigo 2009** that where the job applicant was applying for jobs which she did not actually want, she could not claim to have been discriminated against.

➤ *Case facts*

Ms Keane (K) is an accountant in her late 40s. Via agencies and by herself, she applied for approximately 20 jobs which were only suitable for newly qualified accountants, i.e. she was definitely overqualified. When she failed to get an interview, she would send an age discrimination questionnaire to the employer. Eventually K made eleven claims of age discrimination, six of which were settled (it's estimated that she netted over £100,000). But the EAT recently decided that as K did not really want the jobs, no discrimination could ever have taken place. In other words, she needed to have a genuine desire to do them to suffer a detriment or disadvantage. Furthermore, K was ordered to pay costs.

EMPLOYER TIP

Make sure you have an up-to-date equal opportunities policy and that you provide on-going equal opportunities training for your managers. They will be asked at tribunal if they have undergone this and if the answer is "no" the tribunal will not be impressed.

Download Zone

For an **Equal Opportunities Policy**, visit **http://books.indicator.co.uk**. You'll find the access code on page 2 of this book.

3.1.7. How does a claimant prove they have been discriminated against?

First of all, let's clear up a point that causes confusion. When we talk of "proof" in the tribunal, we do not mean that a person has to prove something happened "beyond all reasonable doubt". That test is only used in criminal courts. In tribunals (and civil courts) a claimant only has to demonstrate "on the balance of probabilities" that something happened, i.e. it is more likely to have occurred than not.

Note. In discrimination cases, the claimant usually gives their evidence first and this should prove, on the balance of probabilities, facts from which the tribunal could conclude that discrimination has occurred. The tribunal must find that this has happened unless the employer can provide a satisfactory, and non-discriminatory, explanation for their conduct. This means that, in practice, it will be for the employer to prove that discrimination did not occur, rather than the claimant proving that it did.

3.1.8. What can we do to prevent a discrimination claim from arising during recruitment?

It's very easy to discriminate unintentionally. To use a simple example, if you said you were seeking "flexibility in working hours" this has the potential to discriminate against women as they may have childcare responsibilities.

But there's a lot that you can do to prevent it. Firstly, when recruiting, always draft a job description and person specification; this will help ensure that there's no unintentional discrimination.

Download Zone

For a **Job Description and Person Specification**, visit **http://books.indicator.co.uk**. You'll find the access code on page 2 of this book.

It's also possible to discriminate at the interview by asking questions which, on the face of it, are innocuous but in reality can discriminate against a particular sector of the population. An example would be asking female candidates if they plan to have a family in the next five years, but not asking the same question of male candidates. Alternatively, it could be asking a man how they will cope in an "all-female" environment. An equal opportunities and dignity at work policy can be used to set out your approach to discrimination and this can be re-iterated in a recruitment policy.

Download Zone

For a **Recruitment Policy**, visit **http://books.indicator.co.uk**. You'll find the access code on page 2 of this book.

Employer tip

When recruiting, retain all documentation for a minimum period of six months, just in case an applicant starts a tribunal claim.

3.1.9. We've received a discrimination questionnaire. Will a tribunal claim follow?

The reason why a claimant would send you such a questionnaire is to obtain information in order to decide whether they should bring a claim of discrimination and, if so, how to present it in the most effective way. See the appendix for a link to the tribunal discrimination questionnaires.

3.1.10. What questions might the claimant ask in a discrimination questionnaire?

If an individual thinks they were discriminated against during the recruitment process, they will typically ask about: **(1)** who was involved in the process; **(2)** statistics relating to certain groups, e.g. women or disabled people, in particular jobs or grades; **(3)** why they were not invited to interview; **(4)** how their qualifications compare with those of the successful candidate; and **(5)** who was appointed to the job.

3.1.11. How are these different to equal pay questionnaires?

An equal pay questionnaire asks for information relating solely to pay; they are generally only used once employment has commenced.

Note. An individual can't simply issue an equal pay claim because the person sitting next to them earns more. There are strict rules they must meet, namely that:

- they are comparing themselves with a member of the opposite sex (the "comparator") and
- their comparator does work which:
  - is the same, or broadly similar, to the work that they do; or
  - has been rated as equivalent under a job evaluation exercise; or
  - is of equal value to the work they do (this allows a person to compare themselves with someone doing an entirely different job).

See the appendix for a link to the tribunal's equal pay questionnaire.

3.1.12. Should we ignore any questionnaires?

Risk. Whilst there's no obligation on you to reply to one, if you decide not to respond to a questionnaire, or if your replies are evasive or equivocal, you will be in trouble; the tribunal is entitled to draw an inference that discrimination did take place, even if it didn't!

Note. If you do respond to a questionnaire, remember that anything you say may be used in evidence against you. So always be very careful as to what you write in your response.

> **EMPLOYER TIP**
>
> A claimant does not have to use the tribunal's official questionnaire form. If they prefer they can send you a letter asking for the information they want.

3.1.13. What should we put in our response?

As each questionnaire will require a response that's tailored to its own particular questions, it's impossible to cover every scenario here. We can, however, give you the following general advice:

- be succinct in your answers
- answer the question that has been asked
- don't volunteer information (sometimes you may realise the claimant has asked the wrong question but don't help them)
- stick to the facts
- if you agree with something, don't be afraid to confirm it
- if you feel a question is too onerous, or even impossible to answer, e.g. they've asked for information going back six years or more, say so
- if you believe they are asking for irrelevant information you can state this
- don't lie - you will be caught out if it goes to tribunal.

Key points

Not everyone can start a tribunal claim:

- they must be an employee, or in some cases a worker
- for the majority of claims, such as unfair dismissal, they must be or have been an employee
- but during the recruitment process applicants are protected from discrimination.

When commencing a claim for discrimination:

- there is no minimum service requirement
- the employer will have to provide a satisfactory explanation for the alleged discrimination
- discrimination questionnaires will indicate that an individual is thinking about a tribunal claim.

Minimise the risk of losing discrimination claims at the recruitment stage by:

- preparing a job description and person specification
- not asking potentially discriminatory questions
- retaining all documentation for at least six months.

3.2. STARTING A TRIBUNAL CLAIM

3.2.1. How is a tribunal claim started?

An individual can do this by going to:

- a solicitor
- Citizens' Advice
- a Free Representation Unit (FRU)
- an HR/employment law consultant.

Or by:

- seeking assistance from their union if they are a member of one
- doing it themselves
- getting a friend or family member to help them.

3.2.2. So they don't need to use a solicitor if they don't want to?

No. In fact, many claimants choose to represent themselves (although this could be because they can't afford to pay for advice). Advice is, however, available from FRU and Citizens' Advice who will sometimes go on to represent a claimant free of charge.

3.2.3. Can they get Legal Aid to go to tribunal?

Neither party can get Legal Aid at an employment tribunal. If, however, an appeal is made to the Employment Appeal Tribunal, they could apply for it then.

Employer tip

Many people have legal expenses insurance added on to their household insurance and this is often used to fund tribunal cases. So don't assume that the cost of paying for legal representation will necessarily deter a person from starting a claim.

3.2.4. What does making a claim entail?

It starts with the claimant completing a Form ET1. See the appendix for a link to a Form ET1.

In summary, it will ask for various personal details such as the claimant's name and address, date of birth, dates of employment, rate of pay and, if employment has ended whether or not they have another job. They will also be asked to provide details of their employer, otherwise known as the "respondent".

They also have to complete details of their claim. This is their opportunity to explain exactly what their complaint is about.

Note. On the ET1, Section 5 deals with unfair and constructive dismissal; Section 6 deals with discrimination; Section 7 relates to redundancy payments; Section 8 any other payments; and Section 9 deals with complaints not covered in the previous sections. The remaining sections cover administrative issues.

Employer tip

A claimant must always use the tribunal's official ET1 form. If not, their claim will be rejected.

3.2.5. Is it true that a claim can be made online?

Yes. In fact, this is the easiest way to submit a claim as it can be filled in on-screen and sent to the tribunal.

Note. A claimant or their representative will often adopt this approach if they are up against the relevant statutory time limit.

3.2.6. How will we know if a claim has been made against us?

The first you will usually know about a claim is when the tribunal sends you a copy of the ET1 together with another form called an ET3.

> **Employer tip**
>
> You will also be sent a booklet giving you more information about tribunal claims generally and how to deal with them.

3.2.7. What is the ET3 used for?

This is the document which you use to set out your response.

Note. You must use the ET3 to present your side of the story. See the appendix for a link to Form ET3.

3.2.8. Which tribunal will deal with the case?

Although there are several tribunals located throughout the country, it will most usually be the one nearest the employer's place of business. However, it's quite possible that, if this particular tribunal is over-stretched, the case will be transferred to another one in that region, although tribunals try to avoid doing this wherever possible.

3.2.9. What happens if the claimant sends the claim to the wrong tribunal?

When someone lodges a claim they have to look at a list provided by the tribunal service to identify which one covers a postcode where they normally worked. They should then send their claim to that tribunal. If they do not do this, e.g. they forward it to their local tribunal, it will be stamped as received (although it's not necessarily accepted at this point) and forwarded on to the correct tribunal.

3.2.10. Is there a time limit for filing a claim?

The nature of the claim will determine how long the limit is. For example, if an employee wishes to claim unfair dismissal, they must lodge their application with the tribunal no later than three months beginning with the "effective date of termination" (EDT).

This will vary according to whether or not the employee works their notice and can be summarised as follows:

- in cases of summary dismissal (for gross misconduct) where no notice is given or pay in lieu of notice is made, the EDT is the dismissal date
- if notice is given and worked by the employee, the EDT is the last day of the notice period
- if payment is made in lieu of notice, the EDT is the date of dismissal.

Where the claim is for discrimination, the time limit is also three months but this starts from the date of the act of discrimination or, where the discrimination comprises a continuing series of acts, from the date that the last alleged incident of discrimination took place.

For all other claims, the time limit is three months, with the exception of equal pay and redundancy payment claims where it is six months.

Employer tip

Employees are often caught out by the three-month period so look out for this. In a case of unfair dismissal, if you dismiss on April 5 the three months expires on July 4 - not July 5. If, on the other hand, the person is claiming that an act of discrimination occurred on April 5, the three months will expire on July 5. So always check they've got their claim in on time - even a few hours could make a difference.

3.2.11. Will a tribunal ever accept a claim outside these limits?

Tribunals do have the discretion to accept late claims but they would only exercise this in exceptional circumstances. Furthermore, the test as to whether or not the claim should be accepted differs according to whether it's for discrimination or, e.g. unfair dismissal.

Employer tip

Tribunals can accept discrimination claims which fall outside the time limit where it would be "just and equitable" to do so. For unfair dismissal and other claims, the tribunal might exercise its discretion where it was "not reasonably practicable" to present the claim in time.

3.2.12. Once a claim is lodged, can the tribunal stop it from going to a full hearing?

Many people think that if a claimant mounts a seemingly hopeless claim the tribunal will somehow step in and prevent it from going any further. In reality, tribunals have limited powers to stop a claim from proceeding.

Firstly, when a claim arrives at the tribunal office, it will be scrutinised to make sure that the tribunal can accept it. At this stage, it will be rejected if there is a procedural error, e.g.:

- an incorrect form has been used
- the claimant does not have sufficient service
- the claim is out of time; or
- the tribunal has no jurisdiction to consider the claim (such as personal injury claims).

In some cases, the tribunal will arrange a "Pre-Hearing Review" at which a judge will assess whether or not the case has any likelihood of succeeding. If it is unlikely to succeed, the claimant can be asked to pay a deposit (maximum £500) which is normally refunded at the end of the hearing.

In addition, a tribunal judge has the power to "strike-out" a claim but this is used sparingly; it means the case can't go ahead. Examples of when a strike-out might be appropriate include cases where:

- the claim is vexatious
- the claim has no reasonable prospect of success
- a representative behaves in a scandalous, unreasonable or vexatious manner
- or where a party has failed to comply with a tribunal order.

3.2.13. How long will it take before the case is heard?

This will very much depend on the type of claim that's being made. A simple one, such as unpaid wages, will often be heard within two or three months. Cases that are more complicated can take over a year until they get a hearing date.

Note. The overall aim of tribunals is to hear all claims within six months of them being lodged and over 90% of claims are heard within this period.

Key points

When making a tribunal claim:

- it can be done either by completing a form and posting it to the tribunal, or online
- a Form ET1 must be used
- claimants do not need to be legally represented
- Legal Aid is not available.

If an ET1 is submitted to the wrong tribunal it will be:

- stamped as received
- sent on to the correct tribunal.

There are strict time limits in the tribunal:

- most claims must be submitted within three months
- for equal pay and redundancy pay claims the time limit is six months
- always check the date the claim is submitted to make sure it's in time
- tribunals have a limited discretion to accept claims outside of these limits.

Tribunals can stop cases from going forward if:

- an incorrect form has been used
- the claimant does not have sufficient service
- the claim is out of time, vexatious, or has no reasonable prospect of success
- a claimant or their representative behaves in a scandalous, unreasonable or vexatious manner
- a party fails to comply with a tribunal order.

Once the tribunal accepts the claim:

- a copy of the ET1 will be sent to the employer together with Form ET3 for the employer to complete
- the employer must use Form ET3 when they respond to the claim
- it will be dealt with by the one nearest to the employer's place of business
- it will aim to deal with it within six months of it being lodged.

3.3. RESPONDING TO THE CLAIM

3.3.1. How do we respond to the claim?

Firstly, your response must be made on the Form ET3. It's also very important that you carefully check all the information provided by the claimant. If you disagree with anything they have stated, now is your opportunity to provide the correct information.

Employer tip

If you submit your ET3 online or by fax, do not send a hard copy to the tribunal office by post. It will merely confuse things!

3.3.2. What will make the claim invalid?

A claim will be invalid if:

- the tribunal has no jurisdiction to hear that particular claim
- it has been lodged outside the time limit - check the date stamp on the front of the ET1 to make sure the claimant is within the time limit.
- the claimant does not have the minimum service required
- the claimant has named the wrong respondent. For example, they are employed by A Company Ltd, which is a subsidiary of B Company Plc, and they name the parent company as their employer. This is a very common mistake.

Note. If you believe that any of the above apply you should draw this to the attention of the tribunal by sending a separate letter explaining why you think the claim is invalid. If it agrees, the claim will be struck out.

Employer tip

Whenever you send correspondence to the tribunal, always refer to the case number and send a copy to the claimant or their representative.

3.3.3. What should our defence include?

Try to be succinct in your response and stick to the facts. Where you accept or agree to something stated by the claimant, acknowledge this, as it will ultimately save time (and money). Only where you dispute a fact should you deny it and also put your version of events.

Don't attempt to write a short story. Take each paragraph and respond to it by simply setting out a brief description of what occurred. For example, the claimant might state that when they were dismissed you did not follow the disciplinary procedure. If you believe that it was followed in full you should state this in your response. If, on the other hand, you know that you didn't follow the procedure, you should concede that it was not complied with - although you might prefer to say that, had it been complied with, the employee would still have been dismissed.

Employer tip

Always number the paragraphs when you set out your defence. This makes it easier for the tribunal to refer to them.

3.3.4. What is the time limit for filing a defence?

Your ET3 must be presented to the tribunal within 28 days from the date on which the tribunal sent you a copy of the claim, i.e. the ET1. This date is the one on the letter telling you that a claim has been made against you.

Note. When calculating the 28 days, disregard the date on the letter and start from the next one. For example, if the ET1 was sent to you on March 1 the last day that you can present your ET3 will be March 29.

Risk. If you fail to present your ET3 in time, it will be rejected and you will not be allowed to take part in the proceedings. The tribunal might also issue a default judgment without holding a hearing. This means not only could you be held liable - in other words you lose your case - but if compensation is awarded, you will have no influence on the amount to be paid.

Employer tip

If you decide to post the ET3 make sure you allow at least two days, excluding Sundays and bank/public holidays. Also, send it by first class post and obtain proof of posting. If you decide to deliver it by hand to the tribunal office, get a dated receipt.

3.3.5. Can we ask for an extension of time?

It is possible to apply for an extension, but you must do this before the end of the 28-day limit. Where you need to apply for an extension you should:

- put your request in writing to the tribunal office, including the case number

- explain, in detail, the reason(s) for your request. For example, if you are unable to obtain all the information because someone is on holiday and they will not return until after the deadline
- advise how an extension would assist the tribunal in dealing fairly with the proceedings, e.g. it will have all the information to hand.

Note. You should also copy this to the claimant who has the right to object to an extension.

3.3.6. What documents should we send with the ET3?

None - not even a covering letter! Any other documentation that you wish to use in relation to the claim should be presented in a "bundle" (more about that later) and taken to the tribunal on the day of the hearing.

3.3.7. Can we alter our response once it has been sent to the tribunal?

Not easily. Any amendments to the ET3 can only be made with the approval of the tribunal. In practice, if such a request is made early on in the proceedings, there will not be a problem and "leave to amend" will be given.

If, however, you wait until the hearing before you ask to amend your response, you may find yourself in difficulty.

Note. Where the amendment would put the claimant at a disadvantage because they did not know you were going to raise it and are unprepared to deal with it, the tribunal is likely to turn down your request.

Employer tip

As soon as you realise that you need to amend your ET3 write to the tribunal explaining what changes you need to make, and why. A copy of this letter must also be sent to the claimant, or their representative.

Key points

When you respond to a claim you must:

- always use the Form ET3
- read and check each section of the ET1 carefully
- ensure you correct any information given on the ET1, such as dates of employment or rate of pay, in your ET3
- not send any other documents.

Your defence should:

- be succinct
- be factual
- identify issues which are not in dispute
- concede anything you know you have done incorrectly.

A 28-day time limit applies for returning the ET3:

- from the date it was sent to you by the tribunal
- which can be found on the accompanying letter
- but the date of posting is disregarded when calculating the period
- and your ET3 will be rejected if you fail to return it on time.

If you need an extension of time you should:

- write to the tribunal and request an extension
- explain why you need the extension
- explain how this will help the tribunal deal fairly with the case
- send a copy of your request to the claimant.

If you need to amend your ET3 you should:

- write to the tribunal as soon as possible
- explain what amendment you would like to make and why
- send a copy to the claimant
- not expect the tribunal to agree.

3.4. ACAS AND THE STATUTORY CONCILIATION PROCESS

3.4.1. What is ACAS?

ACAS stands for the Advisory, Conciliation and Arbitration Service. It has three roles, namely to:

- give free advice to employers and employees, either by phone or online
- conciliate between the parties to a tribunal claim with the objective of agreeing a settlement. A large proportion of cases are settled this way
- arbitrate between an employer and employee if they are in dispute over employment issues and can't resolve the situation themselves.

3.4.2. What is conciliation?

This is where an ACAS officer tries to get the parties to reach a voluntary settlement of the complaint, or potential complaint, once the claimant has already started a claim against the employer. If this is successful, there will be no need for the claim to proceed to a tribunal hearing.

3.4.3. Do we have to pay ACAS for its assistance with conciliation?

No. It offers this service free of charge.

3.4.4. Will ACAS always get involved?

It will attempt to conciliate in most employment claims, for example unfair dismissal, maternity rights, working time claims, TUPE, Sunday working, flexible working, equal pay plus anything to do with discrimination.

There are, however, certain claims it can't deal with. These relate to written particulars of employment and claims to the Secretary of State when an employer becomes insolvent. These latter claims usually arise when employees are seeking redundancy, notice or holiday pay.

3.4.5. When will ACAS contact us?

When a claim has been made to tribunal, a copy of the ET1 and ET3 will be sent to ACAS. The tribunal will also tell you which ACAS office the papers have gone to and you can contact them yourself.

3.4.6. Will ACAS take our side?

No, it is completely impartial; its sole purpose is to get the parties to reach a settlement. However, they are allowed to:

- tell you what the law says
- illustrate this by referring to relevant cases
- explain tribunal procedure
- advise you about the issues which a tribunal will have to consider and what it will take into account
- explain the circumstances in which you could have costs awarded against you should you proceed with your defence
- help you draft any settlement agreement
- assist you in calculating how much compensation might be awarded against you if the claimant is successful.

Employer tip

An ACAS officer will never advise you on how likely you are to win or lose a case. If you are seeking this type of advice, you will have to consult your legal representative.

3.4.7. Do we have to speak to the conciliator?

No. There is no obligation on you to participate in the conciliation process although you should bear in mind that nothing will be lost by at least trying to settle the claim; it is free after all. But the vast majority of claims (over 75%) are settled via ACAS conciliation.

Employer tip

Conciliation can help to identify the real issues and often a claimant will withdraw their claim once the law has been explained to them.

3.4.8. If we settle, must we admit liability?

Not at all. Some employers think that settling is tantamount to admitting that they were in the wrong but nothing could be further from the truth. It is simply a pragmatic way of dealing with a problem, i.e. it stops it hanging over you for eight to twelve months, distracting you from running your business.

3.4.9. Could our representative deal with ACAS on our behalf?

Yes they can. If you've already identified a representative on the ET3, ACAS will automatically contact them.

If, at the time of completing the ET3, you did not have a representative but you appointed one afterwards, you should inform the tribunal, the claimant and ACAS as soon as possible. Negotiations will then take place between ACAS and your representative.

3.4.10. What happens if we refuse to conciliate?

Unless the claimant withdraws their claim (which is unlikely), the case will simply proceed to a hearing and you will have to go to tribunal to defend it.

3.4.11. How does conciliation work?

The usual procedure is for the ACAS officer to initially contact the parties (usually by phone). At this stage the conciliator will explain how conciliation works and that it is free and impartial. There will then be an exploratory discussion to ascertain if a settlement can be reached.

The conciliator will speak to each of the parties - should the employer make an offer, this will be relayed to the claimant. It is then up to the claimant to go back to the conciliator with their response. Quite often, they will suggest a higher figure and "horse-trading" will continue until either a deal is made, or an impasse reached.

Employer tip

It's quite common for employers to offer a commercial settlement simply to get rid of a claim.

3.4.12. Can we attempt conciliation any time up to the tribunal hearing?

Yes and it's quite normal for settlements to be reached at 5.00pm on the day before the hearing is due to take place!

Conciliation is often a case of brinkmanship. Whilst many cases are settled early on in the proceedings, others are not (most usually because the level of compensation can't be agreed).

3.4.13. Will ACAS tell me what figure to offer?

No, they are not allowed to advise you on how much to offer. A conciliator acts as a messenger taking any offer you decide to make to the claimant and reporting their response to you.

3.4.14. If we agree to settle, is it formalised?

Hopefully, you will reach a settlement via conciliation. Once you have done so you should immediately contact the conciliator and give them the details. Once a settlement is reached verbally, the conciliator will contact the tribunal and the claim will be removed from the list.

The conciliator will then formalise the agreement on a form known as a COT3. On this will be details of the settlement. Usually, but not always, this will include a sum of money to be paid to the claimant. It's also quite usual for the parties to agree a reference and, sometimes, the claimant might want an apology.

The COT3 will also state that the claimant accepts the money/reference/apology etc. in full and final settlement of all claims arising out of the termination of their contract of employment and/or claim. It will normally specifically exclude claims relating to the claimant's occupational pension and potential personal injury claims.

Download Zone

For a **Sample Form COT3**, visit **http://books.indicator.co.uk**. You'll find the access code on page 2 of this book.

3.4.15. What are the advantages of conciliation?

The main advantage is that you will not have to attend a tribunal hearing and so your costs should be greatly reduced. If you use a solicitor or barrister to present your case, this can easily cost in excess of £10,000, even if you win! A multi-day case will cost even more. Going to tribunal can be a very expensive business and that's before you factor in any compensation awarded against you.

A settlement via conciliation will also save you time. You have to remember that it can take several days to prepare for even a one-day case. Your representative will have to read and understand all the facts of the case, interview witnesses, prepare their witness statements, put the bundle together, prepare their cross-examination and research the relevant law. This all takes time and you will be paying for this.

Whilst proceedings in an employment tribunal are not as formal as those, say, in the Crown Court, appearing at a tribunal as a lay representative or a witness is extremely stressful. It is not unknown for primary witnesses to be giving their evidence for a day or longer. A settlement will avoid the inevitable anxiety that this will cause over a period of months.

Finally, a settlement is made on your terms and is confidential. An award of compensation made in a tribunal hearing is a matter of public record and could be widely reported in the media.

Employer tip

There is also an incentive for the claimant to conciliate; they may want an agreed reference. Tribunals can't order employers to agree a reference, but such an agreement can be reached through a conciliator.

3.4.16. If we don't settle, can our discussions with ACAS be divulged at the tribunal hearing?

No, and if anyone tries to refer to them, the employment judge will immediately step in and tell them that such matters can't be raised in this forum.

Employer tip

On the ACAS website (see **http://acas.org.uk**) there is a nine-minute video which shows you how the conciliation process works.

Key points

ACAS conciliation is:

- free
- impartial
- confidential
- voluntary.

The conciliation officer will not:

- take the side of either party
- advise on the merits of the case
- recommend, or advise on an offer for settlement.

The conciliation officer can:

- tell you what the law is
- explain the tribunal procedure
- explain the circumstances in which costs may be awarded
- explain what issues the tribunal will take into account when reaching their decision
- help you draft a settlement agreement (COT3).

During the conciliation process:

- copies of the ET1 and ET3 will be sent to ACAS
- a conciliator will contact the claimant and respondent, or their representatives, to discuss the case
- you can refuse to take part at any time
- don't be afraid of offering a "commercial settlement" to get rid of the case
- be prepared to settle at the last minute.
- if an agreement is reached, the conciliator will draft a COT3 and the hearing will be cancelled.

Conciliation should be considered because:

- you should save money
- it should save time
- the settlement will be on your terms
- it will be confidential, i.e. no embarrassing details can be reported by the media.

3.5. USING COMPROMISE AGREEMENTS TO YOUR ADVANTAGE

3.5.1. What is a compromise agreement?

It is a principle of employment law that employees and workers cannot contract out of their statutory rights. Compromise agreements are, however, an exception to this rule.

So where an employer and an employee or worker are in dispute, for example, the employee believes they have been unfairly dismissed or discriminated against, the parties can resolve the matter in "full and final settlement" by entering into a compromise agreement. Once it has been signed this will bring to a halt any claim that has been made to tribunal, or prevent any claim from being made in the future to either the tribunal or civil courts.

3.5.2. When can we use a compromise agreement?

Compromise agreements can be entered into either before or after any type of claim has been lodged at tribunal and there is no need to involve ACAS.

But they can also be used when a dismissal is potentially fair, e.g. an employee is being made redundant and is being offered a non-contractual enhanced redundancy payment.

In essence, they prevent the employee from trying it on to get more money.

EMPLOYER TIP

No money should ever be paid to the employee until a compromise agreement has been signed.

3.5.3. What types of claim can be settled via a compromise agreement?

They can cover claims under:

- the **Employment Rights Act 1996**, e.g. redundancy, unfair dismissal
- all discrimination legislation
- the **Working Time Regulations 1998**
- the **National Minimum Wage Act 1998**
- the **Part-time Workers Regulations 2000**

- the **Fixed-term Employees Regulations 2002**
- the **Information and Consultation of Employees Regulations 2004**
- TUPE
- **Trade Union and Labour Relations (Consolidation) Act I992.**

3.5.4. So can we just draft an agreement and ask the employee to sign it on the spot?

No! The law on compromise agreements is very strict. A document stating that *"the employee accepts £x in full and final settlement of all claims arising from the termination of their employment"* is worthless.

If you want to use a compromise agreement the following conditions must be met:

- the agreement must be in writing
- it must relate to the "particular complaint"
- the employee must have received independent legal advice from a relevant independent advisor as to the terms and effect of the proposed agreement and, in particular, its effect on their ability to pursue their rights in an employment tribunal
- there must be in force, when the advisor gives the advice, a policy of insurance covering the risk of a claim by the employee in respect of loss arising in consequence of the advice; and
- the agreement must identify the advisor
- the agreement must state that the conditions regulating compromise agreements under the relevant Act are satisfied.

Note. A "relevant independent advisor" can only be a: **(1)** a solicitor; **(2)** trade union officer whom the union has certified is competent to give advice; **(3)** advice centre workers who have been certified as being competent to give advice; and **(4)** Fellow of the Institute of Legal Executives (who can also give advice on certain claims in certain circumstances).

Employer tip

The employee must seek legal advice. If they fail to do so, or simply write on the agreement that they didn't want it, the agreement will be invalid and the employee can still pursue a tribunal and/or court claim against you.

3.5.5. Must we pay for their legal advice?

There is no legal obligation on an employer to pay for the legal advice received by the employee. But in practice, most employers will offer a contribution towards this cost simply because it can encourage the employee to enter into the agreement.

Note. In many cases the employee's solicitor will try to force you to pay their client's entire legal bill. You can resist this but, if it's going to make the difference between having the agreement and not having it, do consider if it will make commercial sense to pay.

Employer tip

As a rule of thumb a contribution of around £350 - £400 plus VAT is likely to be offered in London and around £250 - £300 plus VAT elsewhere.

3.5.6. Must employment be terminated for a compromise agreement to exist?

No, there is no requirement for this to happen.

Compromise agreements are particularly useful when employment is terminated but they can also be used to settle other disputes which are ongoing whilst the employee is still employed, e.g. cases involving discrimination or harassment and unlawful deductions from wages.

3.5.7. What are the main advantages of compromise agreements?

They are useful because:

- you can get rid of unwanted employees quickly and relatively painlessly
- they avoid having to deal with tribunal claims
- they will contain a confidentiality clause preventing the employee from publicising the settlement.

Key points

Compromise agreements:

- are a contract between the employer and the employee or worker
- prevent an employee or worker taking a particular claim to tribunal, or stop one that is already lodged
- can be entered into without approaching ACAS.

They can be used:

- to get rid of troublesome employees without going through formal procedures
- to protect an employer who has paid a non-contractual payment
- either before or after a claim has been presented to tribunal.

The agreement must:

- be in writing
- identify the "particular complaint"
- confirm that the employee/worker has received legal advice from a relevant independent advisor
- identify the advisor who must also have insurance
- state that the conditions relating to compromise agreements have been satisfied.

Compromise agreements are advantageous for employers because they:

- allow you to get rid of unwanted employees quickly
- avoid tribunal claims
- will contain a confidentiality clause preventing the employee from publicising the settlement.

3.6. PREPARING FOR A TRIBUNAL HEARING

3.6.1. How much time will we have to prepare for the hearing?

You may have several weeks in which to prepare but it's quite possible that you will only have 14 days' notice; the minimum laid down in law.

Note. The process of fixing a date for the hearing is called "listing" and this will be done by the tribunal dealing with the case. Tribunals are given targets, one of which is to hear cases within 26 weeks. Simple cases, such as a claim for outstanding wages, may be heard within a few weeks. But for more complex ones, and certainly those involving several days' evidence (known as multi-day hearings), you will often have to wait up to six months (sometimes longer) for it to be heard.

3.6.2. Can we ask the tribunal not to list the case for a particular date?

Yes, you can. Sometimes, and particularly for multi-day cases, the tribunal will send you a form asking for the dates when you and your witnesses will be unavailable during the expected hearing period. This is your only opportunity to influence the hearing date, so make sure you immediately contact your witnesses to check their availability. Once you have given the dates to the tribunal it will be very hard, if not impossible, to get the date of the hearing changed.

Note. Sometimes a pre-hearing review (PHR) or case management discussion (CMD) will take place before a case is listed for hearing. A PHR is normally held to clarify the issues and to discourage parties from pursuing a weak case; a CMD will deal with procedural points and case management issues, such as imposing time limits for the exchange of documents. At either of these discussions, it's possible for a hearing date to be agreed between the parties.

EMPLOYER TIP

If you attend a PHR or CMD, make sure you have checked unavailable dates for all of your witnesses so that you can agree a date at the hearing.

3.6.3. What happens if a witness is unavailable for a hearing date?

If you are notified of the hearing date and you find that a witness can't attend, you must write to the tribunal immediately (copying in the claimant), asking for a new date. You must provide a full explanation as to why the given date is inconvenient.

Employer tip

Don't be surprised if the tribunal asks for proof. For example, if an important witness has to attend hospital, you will need to provide a letter or appointment card confirming this. But as long as you do this early enough your request should be granted. However, tribunals are not particularly sympathetic to postponing cases simply because a witness is on holiday; they have been known to order a witness who was on holiday to return early.

3.6.4. How many days will the tribunal allow for the hearing?

It depends on how much evidence it needs to hear. As a guide, the tribunal will expect to hear up to three witnesses in a day, but it is not unknown for a single witnesses to give evidence lasting all day, or for even longer.

Employer tip

If there is no PHR, CMD, or pre-listing form, and you think you will need more than one day for the hearing, write to the tribunal immediately (copying in the claimant) and request that it be listed for longer. Try to give an estimate of how long you will need.

3.6.5. How do we best prepare for the hearing?

As soon as you receive the date of the hearing, tell your witnesses when: **(1)** the hearing will be held; **(2)** where it will be held; and **(3)** the time it will begin. You will then have to sort out which documents you want to produce at the tribunal and prepare your witness statements (see below). Finally, you may have some case law to support your arguments. If so, you will need to take copies along on the day of the hearing.

Employer tip

It's not necessary to send them in advance to the claimant, but you should take five copies to the tribunal hearing - one for you, one for the claimant and one each for the tribunal members.

3.6.6. Must we prepare written witness statements?

Yes. All evidence in tribunals is given by reading a written statement, and these are exchanged between the parties in advance (the tribunal normally orders documents to be exchanged by a set date). So you should sit down with your witnesses and go through their evidence as soon as possible.

Note. It's important that all their evidence is contained in the witness statement. Some tribunals may allow supplementary questions but there is no guarantee this will happen.

Risk. If the tribunal orders parties to prepare and exchange documents by a certain date, you must comply with this. Failure to do so could result in the tribunal striking out your response. This means that you will not be entitled to give evidence at the hearing. It could also award costs against you.

3.6.7. How is a statement set out?

It should confirm the name, address of the witness, and then give the evidence in numbered paragraphs, preferably using double line spacing. The pages should also be numbered.

At the end of the statement, the witness should confirm that the evidence they have given is, to the best of their knowledge and belief, true by signing and dating the statement.

Download Zone

For a **Sample Witness Statement**, visit **http://books.indicator.co.uk**. You'll find the access code on page 2 of this book.

3.6.8. What sort of evidence will be important?

The fact that you are defending the case means that you do not agree with all that the claimant has written in their ET1. Your witnesses will give your side of the story, so you should make sure that their statements cover everything with which you disagree.

In addition to witness statements, you will also have to provide relevant documents. However, tribunals do recognise that it can be difficult to identify what should be included and what should be excluded. Only you can decide, but here is some guidance:

- always include a copy of the claimant's contract
- if you wish to refer to a policy or procedure, which is contained in an employee handbook, just copy the relevant section - not the entire handbook
- include copies of all relevant correspondence, including e-mails
- where the case concerns absence, include copies of the attendance record
- if you have photographic evidence, include it

- if notes have been taken of meetings, include them - typed up where possible. If you also have the handwritten notes on file take these along, in case there is any dispute about the accuracy of the notes.

EMPLOYER TIP

Always take a copy of the employee/staff handbook, any other policies and procedures, as well as the claimant's personnel file with you to tribunal - you might be asked to produce a document that is not in the bundle and returning to your workplace to get it will cause unnecessary delay.

3.6.9. How do we present documents at the tribunal?

Both your documents and those of the claimant will be put together to form a "joint bundle"; this is usually done by the employer. You can't exclude any documents that the claimant wants to put into the bundle - even if they harm your case.

Note. The easiest way of presenting the documents is in chronological order.

Preparing the bundle involves some important rules:

1. Make six copies - one for you, one for the claimant, three for the tribunal and one for the witness table.
2. You must paginate the bundle. This means that you number each page, preferably at the bottom right-hand corner. Do this before you make your six copies or it will take you ages to number them all!
3. Include a contents list at the front of the bundle.

EMPLOYER TIP

Tribunals often complain that bundles are too large; sometimes they run to several hundred pages. In the majority of cases this is unnecessary. Remember, it's the quality of the evidence that's important, not the quantity.

EMPLOYER TIP

A tribunal will be unimpressed if the hearing is delayed because you've failed to paginate the bundle or bring sufficient copies of it. The tribunal will refuse to make copies for you, which means that you will have to find somewhere that can do it for you quickly.

3.6.10. Do tribunals look at the entire bundle?

It's important to understand that a tribunal will not look at any document in the bundle unless you specifically ask a witness to refer to it during the course of their evidence. The best way of doing this is to include page references in the witness statement. For example:

"The employee wrote to the Company on April 1 2010 (page 20 of the bundle) and I replied in a letter dated April 3 2010 (page 21 of the bundle)."

EMPLOYER TIP

Tribunals find that a chronology of events is very useful. Simply list the relevant dates, what happened, together with the page number in the bundle of any document relating to the event. You can present this as a separate document, or include it in the bundle.

3.6.11. Can we present video or audio evidence?

Yes, this should be allowed, but you must write to the tribunal copying in the claimant, warning them that you will want to present such evidence. The tribunal will not provide a TV monitor, video or tape recorder, so you will have to take any relevant equipment with you.

3.6.12. Which documents will the tribunal read before the hearing?

The tribunal will only read the ET1 and ET3 before the hearing and even then only about ten minutes before it's due to start. This is why you must refer them to any documents that you want it to consider, or they will just be ignored.

Key points

Tribunals aim to hear cases within six months and you:

- will get at least 14 days' notice of the hearing date
- can ask the tribunal to avoid inconvenient dates - but it does not have to agree to this
- can notify it if a tribunal date has been listed for an unavoidable event, e.g. a witness is in hospital.

As soon as you have been notified of the hearing date:

- tell your witnesses the date, time and venue of the hearing
- decide which documents you want to produce as evidence
- speak to each witness and prepare a written witness statement
- decide if there is any case law you want to use to support your case.

Witness statements must:

- be typed
- be exchanged with the claimant in advance of the hearing
- not include irrelevant material
- be in the witness's own words.

Relevant evidence can include:

- the contract of employment
- extracts from policies, procedures and employee handbooks
- notes of meetings
- correspondence and e-mails
- photographs, video and tape recordings
- employee attendance records.

Evidence is presented in an agreed bundle that:

- the employer usually prepares
- should ideally start with a contents page
- lists documents in chronological order
- is paginated, i.e. numbered pages
- is copied six times for the hearing.

3.7. AT THE TRIBUNAL HEARING

3.7.1. Who hears the claim?

Straightforward claims, such as those relating to written statements of employment particulars, itemised pay statements, unlawful deductions from pay and redundancy payments can be heard by a single employment judge (who is a barrister or solicitor).

However, the vast majority of claims are heard by a full tribunal that comprises an employment judge and two non-judicial lay members who are appointed because of their experience and knowledge of the workplace. The lay members are not expected to have any legal knowledge (although some do) as they will be guided on the law by the judge.

EMPLOYER TIP

Don't underestimate the influence of lay members - it's not uncommon for them to outvote the judge!

3.7.2. What is it like inside a tribunal?

Unlike other courts, a tribunal room is relatively informal. As you enter, you will normally see a slightly raised platform where the tribunal panel members sit at a long table. At each side of this, there will be a small table. One is where the witnesses sit to give their evidence; the other is used by the tribunal clerk. Facing the tribunal are long tables at which the parties and/or their representatives sit. Behind them are rows of chairs for witnesses, public observers and journalists.

3.7.3. Can we visit a tribunal?

If you, or any of your witnesses have not been to an employment tribunal before, it's a good idea to visit one. If you go to the tribunal website (see **http://employmenttribunals.gov.uk**) you can find out which one is nearest to you.

EMPLOYER TIP

Tribunals sit from 10.00a.m. until approximately 4.30p.m. You should arrive prior to 10.00a.m. and explain to the receptionist that you would like to sit in on a case as you need to understand how a tribunal conducts a hearing. Once inside the tribunal, you are free to leave at any time.

3.7.4. Are the press allowed in to hear a case?

Yes, members of the media are entitled to attend tribunal hearings. The only exception is when the hearing is being held in private but this does not occur very often. An example of this might be where a public hearing might jeopardise national security.

Although the media can attend tribunal hearings, they are rarely present. The cases most likely to attract media attention are those relating to discrimination, particularly sex discrimination, as well as those concerning large employers, or who are well known in the area.

Media interest is a two-edged sword. Obviously if you lose, you can look forward to details of your employment practices being plastered over the press. On the other hand, if you win, such publicity could be welcome, as it could deter other employees from going to tribunal in the future.

3.7.5. Will the case definitely go ahead and finish on time?

There is no guarantee that your case will be heard on the day it is listed as, unfortunately, some are listed as "floating cases". This means that your case will only go ahead once a previous one has finished. It's also possible that you will be there until well after lunchtime only to be told that you will have to go away and come back another day.

But if it does start on time, whether or not it will be finished by the end of the allotted time will depend on whether you and the other party allowed sufficient days for the hearing to be completed.

3.7.6. What happens if the case is not completed on time?

This will mean that the hearing is adjourned and a new date fixed for it to continue - this is known as "going part-heard". The problem is that this could be months into the future because you have to find a date when the three tribunal members, as well as the parties and their representatives, are available. This helps nobody as memories fade over time. It is far better, therefore, to err on the side of caution and ask for a day longer than you think you will need when you are asked about the matter being listed for hearing.

Employer tip

When you calculate the number of days required for the hearing don't forget that the tribunal must be able to make its decision in the allotted time too. Decision-making can take a day or more on its own, and if a remedy is awarded it may be necessary to hear more evidence on the steps the claimant has taken to find alternative employment.

3.7.7. Will we get a decision on the day the hearing finishes?

Not always, although tribunals do try very hard to give a decision (judgment) on the day, as they recognise that the parties need to know the outcome. Sometimes, however, time will be short and it will not be possible to properly consider the evidence and give a judgment on the day. In this situation tribunals "reserve" their decision and you will be informed, in writing, of the outcome.

Note. This can take several weeks - another reason to make sure you have allowed sufficient time for the hearing.

3.7.8. Will we get a written copy of the judgment?

Unless the decision is reserved, an oral judgment, together with reasons for it will be given at the hearing. The judgment will then be confirmed in writing but this will not include written reasons unless you ask for them.

Employer tip

If you are considering an appeal, you will definitely need written reasons. You can either ask for them at the hearing, or within 14 days of the date when the judgment was sent to the parties.

3.7.9. If we lose, will compensation be decided on the same day?

This will depend on how much time is available. If time is short, the tribunal will arrange another hearing, known as a "remedies hearing". A date for this might not be found for several months. However, this does present an opportunity for the parties to sort out compensation between themselves and many remedies hearings are cancelled as a result.

3.7.10. Must we be represented?

No, and many employers who represent themselves do go on to win - mainly because they know the case inside out. But if the case is complex, you might prefer to be represented either by a specialist employment lawyer or HR practitioner who has solid experience of tribunal work.

3.7.11. If we represent ourselves, will that put us at a disadvantage?

Not necessarily. The tribunal simply wants the facts of the case put succinctly, and you are in as good a position to provide these as any solicitor would be. On the other hand, if the case concerns a particularly difficult area of the law, then you may well be at a disadvantage if the other side has legal representation.

Employer tip

You can always seek initial advice from a solicitor who can point you in the right direction and then present the case yourself.

3.7.12. If we choose to be represented, must this person be legally qualified?

No. Whilst the majority of employers will use their own solicitors (who may then appoint a specialist employment barrister to undertake the hearing) you may prefer to use the legal services of any trade organisation to which you might belong, or an HR/employment law consultant. It's entirely up to you.

3.7.13. If we start defending the case ourselves, can we decide to use a solicitor later?

This is perfectly acceptable but do remember to write to the tribunal, and the claimant, and give them details of your new representative. You also need to remember that, once you have done this, all future correspondence will be sent to your representative and not to you.

3.7.14. What is hearsay evidence?

This is probably best explained by giving an example:

Whilst giving his evidence, Brian, says: *"Peter told me that John had said to him that the security gate had been left open all night."*

Brian is simply repeating something which was said to someone else. He has no way of proving that the statement made to Peter is true (unless, of course, Peter is also present to give evidence and confirms this).

Tribunals are wary of hearsay evidence. Apart from the fact that the witness can't prove what they have said, the maker of the statement is not usually available to be cross-examined. Therefore, you should avoid the use of hearsay evidence as it will be disregarded by the tribunal.

3.7.15. Can a witness be forced to attend if they initially refuse?

In this situation, you can apply to the tribunal for a "witness order", known as a "sub-poena" in other courts. But we would advise you to think very carefully before requesting one. This is because once the witness turns up you will have no control over what they might say, i.e. you don't know whether their evidence will help or hinder your case until they start speaking. Unless absolutely necessary, do not go down this route.

If you decide that it's vital, you should write to the tribunal at least ten days before the hearing providing the:

- name and address of the witness
- details of the evidence which you expect them to give
- reason(s) why you need a witness order.

You must also send a copy of your letter to the claimant.

Note. There is no guarantee that a tribunal will grant a witness order but, if the judge believes that the evidence which might be given is relevant and the witness will not attend unless a witness order is made, it will usually be granted.

3.7.16. If a witness does not attend will the tribunal still read their statement?

Tribunals do have discretion to accept written statements in the absence of a live witness but it will attach very little weight to this, as the witness is not present to be cross-examined.

3.7.17. If a major witness is ill on the day of the hearing, can we ask for a postponement?

It is possible to ask for a postponement (if the case has not yet started) or an adjournment (if you are making the application on the day of the hearing). However, the tribunal will want proof, i.e. you will have to provide a medical certificate.

3.7.18. Can we still settle once we turn up at tribunal?

You can settle at any time before the tribunal gives their decision and it's extremely common for the parties to settle while they are waiting to be called into the tribunal. Tribunals encourage settlements - after all, if your case goes away, it means another case can be heard.

If your case has not yet started, and you think it might settle, ask the tribunal clerk to report the situation to the tribunal and request some extra time for further negotiations to take place. This should be granted, but don't expect the tribunal to sit around all morning on the off-chance that you might settle. Initially, you might be given half an hour, with an instruction to let the clerk know how you are progressing.

Note. Sometimes during the hearing one of the parties might decide that a settlement would be in their best interests. Should this be the case, you can ask the tribunal for an "adjournment" in order to speak to the other side. Again, such a request will usually be granted.

Employer tip

Tribunals have been known to drop heavy hints regarding settlements. For example, if the judge asks the parties if they would like an adjournment to discuss the case, this is usually code for *"we think you should go away and settle"*.

3.7.19. Are the panel members influenced by appearance and demeanour?

There is no doubt that tribunals are influenced by the appearance and demeanour of a witness. This doesn't mean that all witnesses have to wear a suit, or collar and tie, although this is advisable. It is more to do with a person's body language. A witness who sits upright and looks directly at the tribunal panel when answering questions will create a better impression than a witness who lolls in the witness chair and appears to be treating the proceedings as a joke.

3.7.20. What could irritate the panel?

At all costs, you should avoid failing to:

- turn up on schedule as it cuts into the time allowed for the hearing. If you are likely to be late, e.g. unexpected delays on public transport, telephone the tribunal office and explain why. There is no obligation on a tribunal to contact you and the case could proceed in your absence, which means you could lose
- produce sufficient copies of the bundle - you will have to go off and find somewhere to photocopy it for you and this wastes time and will cost you money
- number the pages in the bundle

- produce written witness statements - tribunals may allow you to give oral evidence but it won't improve their mood as it will take longer to hear the evidence! It will also put the other party at an advantage
- prepare your case properly, e.g. not having important documents readily available
- listen to, and comply with, instructions and comments from the judge. If you are told that the tribunal really does not need to know something, don't pursue it
- answer the question that has been asked.

Also likely to annoy them is:

- conducting an aggressive cross-examination, intimidating or bullying a witness
- repeating a point time and time again because you have not got the answer you were looking for - just move on to the next issue
- making statements instead of asking questions during cross-examination
- being unpleasant to the tribunal clerk outside of the hearing - they will complain to the tribunal panel about the behaviour of parties.

3.7.21. If we win, can we ask for costs?

Yes, but they will only be awarded in certain strictly-defined circumstances, namely, where:

- the other party or its representative has acted vexatiously, abusively, disruptively or otherwise unreasonably by bringing the proceedings
- the bringing or conducting of the proceedings by a party has been misconceived
- a party has not complied with an order or direction
- a party was ordered to pay a deposit at a pre-hearing review.

Note. Costs can only be awarded to a legally represented claimant and are at the discretion of the tribunal. A party who is not legally represented can apply for a "preparation time costs order". This will compensate for the time taken to prepare for the case but not attendance at the tribunal; it's calculated at around £25 - £30 per hour. One, or more, of the circumstances set out above must apply to an application for preparation time costs.

It should be emphasised that an award of costs still remains quite a rare occurrence and, in order to succeed, a respondent will have to persuade the tribunal that either the claimant has acted unreasonably in the conduct of the proceedings, or that the case was misconceived from the outset and should never have been commenced. In addition, the tribunal will take into account a party's ability to pay.

3.7.22. How much can be awarded for our costs?

The intention is to compensate a party for their costs incurred in bringing, or defending the case. Evidence will, therefore, have to be produced as to the amount being claimed, e.g. a detailed breakdown of your legal representative's fees; you can't simply ask for a particular sum of money.

A tribunal can then award costs as follows:

- it can order payment of a sum not exceeding £10,000
- where the parties have agreed a sum, the order will be for that amount
- the sum can be assessed by the county court - this would be normal where the amount claimed exceeds £10,000.

3.7.23. If we lose, can we appeal?

You can't appeal against a decision simply because you are unhappy with it; appeals can only be made on a point of law. For example, the tribunal:

- did not ask itself the right legal questions
- applied the wrong legal test(s)
- ignored a binding precedent
- misunderstood or misinterpreted the law
- failed to give adequate reasons for its decision
- was biased towards the other party
- identified facts that were not supported by the evidence
- came to a "perverse" decision, i.e. one which no reasonable tribunal could have reached after properly applying the relevant law.

KEY POINTS

Tribunal cases can:

- be heard by a judge sitting alone, or by a full tribunal comprised of three members
- be heard in public and anyone can attend
- allow an adjournment so that the parties can explore a settlement.

Tribunals are:

- influenced by witness demeanour
- easily annoyed, e.g. by lateness, failure to have sufficient bundles etc.
- able to order a witness to attend if they are refusing
- unlikely to attach much weight to a statement if a witness is not present
- only able to award costs as an exception rather than the rule
- known to drop "heavy hints" that the parties should settle.

Appeals can only be made on a point of law, for example the tribunal:

- ignored a binding precedent
- misunderstood or misinterpreted the law
- failed to give adequate reasons for its decision
- was biased towards another party
- identified facts not supported by the evidence.

3.8. COMMON CONCERNS

3.8.1. Is it true that we have to make opening and closing submissions? If so, what are they?

These submissions are simply your opportunity to introduce and close the case. However, it's rare for a tribunal to hear opening submissions; most of the time it will just ask the parties to call their first witness.

On the other hand, most parties will make closing submissions in which they can summarise the main points and arguments of their case.

EMPLOYER TIP

Some legal representatives draft a "skeleton argument" which they then use as a framework for their submissions. A copy of it is given to the tribunal and the other side. Preparing this in advance gives you the opportunity to give some thought to your submissions rather than thinking on your feet at the end of the hearing. Remember that not all tribunals allow representatives time to prepare their submissions; they are expected to follow on from the last witness, so a skeleton will help you.

3.8.2. We're worried about conducting cross-examination. What should we do?

The purpose of cross-examination is to test, discredit and (hopefully) destroy the evidence of the claimant, or one of their witnesses. Legally qualified representatives are very skilled at this but don't let that put you off.

The secret lies in your preparation and the way you formulate questions. It would be impossible to learn the art in-depth in a few sentences but the following will help you:

- go through each statement line by line and identify anything you do not agree with
- write out the questions that you want to put to them in advance
- ideally, use a lined exercise book with the question on one page and the answer that they give on the opposite page
- keep your questions short. Long questions will confuse the witness and possibly the tribunal panel
- despite your best efforts, a witness may not give you the answer that you want to hear (even one of your own). In this case, move on to the next question
- the idea is to cast doubt over what they are saying, not get them to "confess" that they are wrong.

Employer tip

If your own witnesses have not yet given evidence and it contains disputed facts, make sure that you put this to the claimant and/or their witness, giving them the chance to comment on it. For example:

You: "So, you say that you did not visit Mr Gregg at home?"

Witness: "No, I didn't. I don't even know where he lives."

You: "That's interesting, as Mr Gregg's wife will be giving evidence later to say that she recognises you as the person who came to the house. What do you say to that?"

Employer tip

It may be hard to believe, but the judge has to write longhand notes of everything that's said during a hearing. You should, therefore, keep an eye on the judge's pen and when your witnesses are giving evidence remind them not to speak too fast.

3.8.3. How do we request a break?

Just ask the tribunal for a comfort break.

Employer tip

You will probably find that the tribunal will break during the morning for 10-15 minutes. Afternoon breaks are uncommon, as the tribunal doesn't sit for so long.

3.8.4. Our witness has a physical disability, what should we do?

Ideally, this should be brought to the attention of the tribunal in good time before the hearing (in writing) in case any adjustments need to be made. You should also ensure that the clerk and the tribunal panel are aware of this fact on the day of the hearing.

3.8.5. Our witness does not speak good English, can we bring an interpreter?

In this case, you should write to the tribunal and ask that it arrange to provide an interpreter. You will not be allowed to use your own as this individual must be someone who is independent of the parties.

Note. The same applies if the witness is deaf and needs a sign-language interpreter.

Key points

The purpose of cross-examination is to discredit the evidence of the claimant, so:

- spend sufficient time preparing your cross-examination
- keep questions short and succinct
- if you don't get the answer you want, move on to the next question.

As there is no technology to record what is said:

- the judge has to write everything out long-hand
- watch the judge's pen
- remind your witnesses not to speak too fast.

When it comes to submissions:

- it's rare to have opening ones
- closing ones are recommended - use a skeleton argument
- keep them concise and to the point
- it's not necessary to provide copies of case law to support every argument that you want to make.

The tribunal won't be annoyed if:

- you need a comfort break - just ask for a brief adjournment
- if a witness is disabled and needs to have special arrangements made
- a witness' first language is not English, or they are deaf - alert the tribunal as early as possible to the fact that you will need an (independent) interpreter.

APPENDIX - USEFUL LINKS

Form ET1 - application to an Employment Tribunal

http://www.employmenttribunals.gov.uk/Documents/FormsGuidance/newforms/ET1.pdf

Form ET3 - respondent's response to ET1

http://www.employmenttribunals.gov.uk/Documents/FormsGuidance/newforms/ET3_7_4.pdf

Equality and Human Rights Commission - key legislation

http://www.equalityhumanrights.com/advice-and-guidance/information-for-advisers/key-legislation/

DL56 Disability questionnaire

http://www.equalityhumanrights.com/uploaded_files/dl56_questionnaire.pdf

RR65 Race discrimination questionnaire

http://www.equalityhumanrights.com/uploaded_files/rr65_questionnaire.pdf

SD74 Sex discrimination questionnaire

http://www.equalityhumanrights.com/uploaded_files/sd74_questionnaire.doc

Equal pay questionnaire

http://www.equalityhumanrights.com/uploaded_files/equalpay_questionnaire.doc

CHAPTER 4

Documents

DISCIPLINARY PROCEDURE

Whilst the Company does not intend to impose unreasonable rules of conduct on its employees, certain standards of behaviour are necessary to maintain good employment relations and discipline in the interest of all employees. The Company prefers that discipline be voluntary and self-imposed and in the great majority of cases this is how it works. However, from time to time, it may be necessary for the Company to take action towards individuals whose level of behaviour or performance is unacceptable.

This disciplinary procedure is entirely non-contractual and does not form part of an employee's contract of employment.

Minor faults will be dealt with informally through counselling and training. However, in cases where informal discussion with the employee does not lead to an improvement in conduct or performance or where the matter is considered to be too serious to be classed as minor, for example, unauthorised absences, persistent poor timekeeping, sub-standard work performance, etc. the following disciplinary procedure will be used. At all stages of the procedure, an investigation will be carried out.

The Company will notify the employee in writing of the allegations against him or her and will invite the employee to a disciplinary hearing to discuss the matter. The Company will provide sufficient information about the alleged misconduct or poor performance and its possible consequences to enable the employee to answer the case. This will include the provision of copies of written evidence, including witness statements, where appropriate.

Having given the employee reasonable time to prepare their case, a formal disciplinary hearing will then take place, conducted by a manager, at which the employee will be given the chance to state his or her case, accompanied if requested by a trade union official or a fellow employee of his or her choice. The employee must make every effort to attend the hearing. At the hearing, the employee will be allowed to set out their case and answer any allegations and will also be given a reasonable opportunity to ask questions, present evidence, call relevant witnesses and raise points about any information provided by witnesses.

Following the hearing, the Company will decide whether or not disciplinary action is justified and, if so, the employee will be informed in writing of the Company's decision in accordance with the stages set out below and notified of his or her right to appeal against that decision. It should be noted that an employee's behaviour is not looked at in isolation but each incident of misconduct is regarded cumulatively with any previous occurrences.

Stage 1: Written warning

The employee will be given a formal WRITTEN WARNING. He or she will be advised of the reason for the warning, how he or she needs to improve their conduct or performance, the timescale over which the improvement is to be achieved, that the warning is the first stage of the formal disciplinary procedure and the likely consequences if the terms of the warning are not complied with. The written warning will be recorded but nullified after six months, subject to satisfactory conduct and performance.

Stage 2: Final written warning

Failure to improve performance in response to the procedure so far, a repeat of misconduct for which a warning has previously been issued, or a first instance of serious misconduct or serious poor performance, will result in a FINAL WRITTEN WARNING being issued. This will set out the nature of the misconduct or poor performance, how he or she needs to improve their conduct or performance, the timescale over which the improvement is to be achieved and warn that dismissal will probably result if the terms of the warning are not complied with. This final written warning will be recorded but nullified after twelve months, subject to satisfactory conduct and performance. However, the Company reserves the right to extend the validity of the final written warning to a maximum of three years in cases of very serious misconduct or where the employee has a history of misconduct issues.

Stage 3: Dismissal

Failure to meet the requirements set out in the final written warning will normally lead to DISMISSAL with appropriate notice. A decision of this kind will only be made after the fullest possible investigation. Dismissal can be authorised only by a senior manager or a Director. The employee will be informed of the reasons for dismissal, the appropriate period of notice, the date on which his or her employment will terminate and how the employee can appeal against the dismissal decision.

Gross misconduct

Offences under this heading are so serious that an employee who commits them will normally be summarily dismissed. In such cases, the Company reserves the right to dismiss without notice of termination or payment in lieu of notice. Examples of gross misconduct include:

- any breach of the criminal law, such as theft and unauthorised possession of Company property, fraud, deliberate falsification of records or any other form of dishonesty
- wilfully causing harm or injury to another employee, physical violence, bullying or grossly offensive behaviour

- deliberately causing damage to the Company's property
- causing loss, damage or injury through serious carelessness or gross negligence
- wilful refusal to obey a reasonable management instruction or serious insubordination
- incapacity at work through an excess of alcohol or drugs
- a serious breach of health and safety rules
- harassing, bullying or victimising another employee on the grounds of race, colour, ethnic origin, nationality, national origin, religion or belief, sex, sexual orientation, gender reassignment, marital or civil partnership status, age and/or disability.

The above is intended as a guide and is not an exhaustive list.

Suspension

In the event of serious or gross misconduct, an employee may be suspended on full basic pay while a full investigation is carried out. Such suspension does not imply guilt or blame and will be for as short a period as possible. Suspension is not considered a disciplinary action.

Appeals

An employee may appeal against any disciplinary decision, including dismissal, to a Director of the Company within five working days of the decision. Appeals should be made in writing and state the grounds for appeal. The employee will be invited to attend an appeal hearing chaired by a senior manager or a Director.

At the appeal hearing, the employee will again be given the chance to state his or her case and will have the right to be accompanied by a trade union official or a fellow employee of his or her choice.

Following the appeal hearing, the employee will be informed in writing of the appeal decision. The Company's decision on an appeal will be final.

Employees who have been employed for less than one year

This disciplinary procedure does not apply to any employee who has been employed by the Company for less than one year.

CAPABILITY PROCEDURE

The primary aim of this procedure is to provide a framework within which the Company can work with employees to maintain satisfactory performance standards and to encourage improved performance where necessary. The Company recognises the difference between a deliberate or careless failure on the part of an employee to perform to the standards of which they are capable (in which case the Company will use the disciplinary procedure) and a case of incapability, where the employee is lacking in knowledge, skill or ability and so cannot perform to the standard required (in which case the Company will use this capability procedure in an attempt to improve the employee's performance).

The Company also recognises that during an employee's employment capability to carry out their duties may deteriorate. This can be for a number of reasons; the most common ones being that either the job changes over a period of time and the employee fails to keep pace with the changes or the employee changes and can no longer cope with the work.

This capability procedure is entirely non-contractual and does not form part of an employee's contract of employment.

Minor capability issues will be dealt with informally through counselling and training. Informal discussions may be held with a view to clarifying the required work standards and the level of performance expected of the employee, identifying areas of concern, establishing the likely causes of poor performance, identifying any training or supervision needs, setting targets for improvement and agreeing a timescale for review. However, in cases where informal discussion with the employee does not lead to a satisfactory improvement in performance, or where the performance issues are more serious, the following capability procedure will be used. At all stages of the procedure, an investigation will be carried out.

At all stages the Company will give consideration to whether the unsatisfactory performance is related to a disability and, if so, whether there are any reasonable adjustments that could be made to the requirements of the employee's job or other aspects of the working arrangements.

The Company will notify the employee in writing of the concerns over performance and will invite the employee to a performance review meeting to discuss the matter. The Company will provide sufficient information about the poor performance and its possible consequences to enable the employee to prepare to answer the case. This will include the provision of copies of written evidence where appropriate.

Having given the employee reasonable time to prepare their case, a formal capability meeting will then take place, conducted by a manager, at which the employee will be given the chance to state their case, accompanied if requested by a trade union official or a fellow employee of their choice. The employee must make every effort to attend the meeting.

The purposes of the performance review meeting include: to set out the required standards that the Company considers the employee has not met, to establish the likely causes of poor performance (including any reasons why any measures taken so far have not led to the required improvement) and to allow the employee the opportunity to explain the poor performance and to ask any relevant questions. Except in the case where dismissal is proposed, the purposes of the performance review meeting also include: to discuss measures, such as additional training or supervision, which may improve the employee's performance, to set targets for improvement and to set a reasonable timescale for review (reflecting the circumstances of the case). In a case where dismissal is proposed, the purposes of the performance review meeting also include: to establish whether there are any further steps that could reasonably be taken to rectify the employee's poor performance, to establish whether there is any reasonable likelihood of the required standards of performance being met within a reasonable time and to discuss whether there is any practical alternative to dismissal, such as redeployment to any suitable available job at the same or lower grade.

Following the performance review meeting, the Company will decide whether or not formal performance action is justified and, if so, the employee will be informed in writing of the Company's decision in accordance with the stages set out below and notified of their right to appeal against that decision.

Stage 1: Performance warning

The employee will be given a formal PERFORMANCE WARNING. This will set out the areas in which the employee has not met the required performance standards, targets for improvement, any measures, such as additional training or supervision, which will be taken with a view to improving the employee's performance, a timescale for review and the likely consequences of failing to improve to the required standards within the review period. The performance warning will be recorded but nullified after six months, subject to satisfactory performance.

The employee's performance will be monitored and, at the end of the review period, the Company will write to the employee to advise him or her of the next step. If the Company is satisfied with the employee's performance, no further action will be taken. If the Company is not satisfied with the employee's performance, the matter may be progressed to Stage 2 or, if the Company feels that there has been a substantial but insufficient improvement, the review period may be extended.

Stage 2: Final performance warning

Failure to improve performance in response to the procedure so far, or a first instance of serious poor performance, will result in a FINAL PERFORMANCE WARNING being issued. This will set out the areas in which the employee has still not met the required performance standards, targets for improvement, any further measures, such as additional training or supervision, which will be taken with a view to improving the employee's performance, a further timescale for review and the likely consequences of failing to improve to the required standards within the further review period, i.e. that dismissal will probably result. The final performance warning will be recorded but nullified after twelve months, subject to satisfactory performance.

The employee's performance will again be monitored and, at the end of the further review period, the Company will write to the employee to advise them of the next step. If the Company is satisfied with the employee's performance, no further action will be taken. If the Company is not satisfied with the employee's performance, the matter may be progressed to Stage 3 or, if the Company feels that there has been a substantial but insufficient improvement, the review period may be extended.

Stage 3: Dismissal

Failure to improve performance in response to the procedure so far will normally lead to DISMISSAL, with appropriate notice. The Company may first consider redeploying the employee with their agreement to another available job at the same or lower grade which is more suited to their abilities. A dismissal decision will only be made after the fullest possible investigation. Dismissal can be authorised only by a senior manager or a Director. The employee will be informed of the reasons for dismissal, the appropriate period of notice, the date on which their employment will terminate and how the employee can appeal against the dismissal decision.

Appeals

An employee may appeal against any decision under this capability procedure, including dismissal, to a Director of the Company within five working days of the decision. Appeals should be made in writing and state the grounds for appeal. The employee will be invited to attend an appeal meeting chaired by a senior manager or a Director.

At the appeal meeting, the employee will again be given the chance to state their case and will have the right to be accompanied by a trade union official or a fellow employee of their choice.

Following the meeting, the employee will be informed in writing of the appeal decision. The Company's decision on an appeal will be final.

Employees who have been employed for less than one year

This capability procedure does not apply to any employee who has been employed by the Company for less than one year.

GRIEVANCE PROCEDURE

Policy

The primary purpose of this grievance procedure is to enable staff to air any concerns that they may have about practices, policies or treatment from other individuals at work or from the Company, and to produce a speedy resolution where genuine problems exist. It is designed to help all employees to take the appropriate action, when they are experiencing difficulties, in an atmosphere of trust and collaboration.

Although it may not be possible to solve all problems to everyone's complete satisfaction, this policy forms an undertaking by the Company that it will deal objectively and constructively with all employee grievances, and that anyone who decides to use the procedure may do so with the confidence that their problem will be dealt with fairly.

This grievance procedure is not a substitute for good day-to-day communication in the Company where we encourage employees to discuss and resolve daily working issues in a supportive atmosphere. Many problems can be solved on an informal footing very satisfactorily if all employees are prepared to keep the channels of communication between themselves open and working well. This procedure is designed to deal with those issues that need to be approached on a more formal basis so that every route to a satisfactory solution can be explored and so that any decisions reached are binding and long lasting.

This grievance procedure is entirely non-contractual and does not form part of an employee's contract of employment.

Procedure

If you cannot settle your grievance informally, you should raise it formally. This procedure has been drawn up to establish the appropriate steps to be followed when pursuing and dealing with a formal grievance.

Stage 1

In the event of your having a formal grievance relating to your employment you should, in the first instance, put your grievance in writing and address it to your line manager, making clear that you wish to raise a formal grievance under the terms of this procedure. Where your grievance is against your line manager, your complaint should be addressed to an alternative manager or to the human resources department. This grievance procedure will not be invoked unless you raise your grievance in accordance with these requirements.

A manager (who may not be the manager to whom your grievance was addressed) will then invite you to attend a grievance meeting to discuss your grievance and you have the right to be accompanied at this meeting by a trade union official or a fellow employee of your choice. Every effort will be made to convene the grievance meeting at a time which is convenient for you and your companion to attend. If this means that the meeting cannot be held within a reasonable period (usually within five working days of the original date set), we ask that you make arrangements with another companion who is available to attend. Any employee who is chosen to accompany another in a grievance hearing is entitled to take paid time off for this purpose.

You must make every effort to attend the grievance meeting. At the meeting, you will be permitted to explain your grievance and how you think it should be resolved.

Following the meeting, the Company will endeavour to respond to your grievance as soon as possible and, in any case, within five working days of the grievance meeting. If it is not possible to respond within this time period, you will be given an explanation for the delay and be told when a response can be expected. You will be informed in writing of the Company's decision on the grievance and notified of your right to appeal against that decision if you are not satisfied with it.

Stage 2

In the event that you feel your grievance has not been satisfactorily resolved, you may then appeal in writing to a Director of the Company within five working days of the grievance decision. You should also set out the grounds for your appeal.

On receipt of your appeal letter, a more senior manager or a Director (who again may not be the person to whom your appeal was addressed) shall make arrangements to hear your grievance at an appeal meeting and at this meeting you may again, if you wish, be accompanied by a trade union official or a fellow employee of your choice.

You must make every effort to attend the grievance appeal meeting.

Following the meeting, the senior manager or Director will endeavour to respond to your grievance as soon as possible and, in any case, within five working days of the appeal hearing. If it is not possible to respond within this time period, you will be given an explanation for the delay and be told when a response can be expected. You will be informed in writing of the Company's decision on your grievance appeal.

This is the final stage of the grievance procedure and the Company's decision shall be final.

Disciplinary issues

If your complaint relates to your dissatisfaction with a disciplinary, performance review or dismissal decision, you should not invoke the grievance procedure but should instead appeal against that decision in accordance with the appeal procedure with which you will have been provided.

NOTIFICATION OF DISCIPLINARY HEARING

Date . . . . *(insert date)*

Dear . . . . *(insert name of employee)*

The Company is considering taking disciplinary action against you. You are therefore required to attend a disciplinary hearing on . . . . *(insert date - which should be at least three days after the date of the letter)* at . . . . *(insert time)* at . . . . *(insert location)*. This gives you reasonable time to prepare your case.

A full investigation of the facts surrounding the complaint(s) against you was made by . . . . *(insert name)*. Having now completed that investigation, the allegations against you are as follows:

- *(List each of the allegations in full detail.)*

(Where discipline is for potential gross misconduct:) [In the Company's view, these allegations constitute gross misconduct.]

For your information, copies of the following documents are enclosed:

- *(List copies of all witness statements (which should be signed and dated) and any other supporting documentary evidence that the employer intends to produce and rely on at the disciplinary hearing.)*

These documents form the basis for the Company's complaint(s) and the Company will therefore rely on these documents in support of the allegations made against you.

If you would like to submit a written statement for consideration in advance of the hearing, you may do so. This should be forwarded to . . . . *(insert name)*. At the hearing, you will of course be given the full opportunity to explain your case and answer the allegations. You may ask questions, dispute the evidence, provide your own evidence and otherwise argue your case. You may also put forward any mitigating factors that you consider relevant to your case. Due consideration will be given to any factors or explanations which you raise when considering what, if any, disciplinary sanctions are to be imposed.

The disciplinary hearing will be chaired by . . . . *(insert name)*, and . . . . *(insert name)* will also be present to take an attendance note of the hearing.

You have the statutory right to be accompanied at the disciplinary hearing. Your companion may be either a work colleague or a trade union official of your choice. Your companion will be permitted both to address the hearing (but not to answer questions on your behalf) and to confer with you during the hearing. You should inform the chair of the hearing in advance of the identity of your chosen companion.

(Where the employee already has an active final written warning on file:) [As you already have an active final written warning on your personnel file, I must inform you that the outcome of this disciplinary hearing could result in your dismissal.]

(Where discipline is for potential gross misconduct:): [Since the Company views the allegations against you as gross misconduct, I must inform you that the outcome of this disciplinary hearing could result in your summary dismissal.]

If you or your chosen companion is unable to attend this disciplinary hearing, you are asked to contact. . . . . *(insert name of contact)* as a matter of urgency so that an alternative date and time can be scheduled. You should take all reasonable steps to attend the hearing. Failure to attend without good reason could result in the hearing being held, and a decision being taken, in your absence.

After the disciplinary hearing, you will be informed in writing of the Company's decision.

Yours sincerely

. . . .

For and on behalf of the Company

Enc

NOTICE OF PERFORMANCE REVIEW MEETING

Date . . . . *(insert date)*

Dear . . . . *(insert name of employee)*

The Company is considering instituting performance review action against you on the ground of a lack of capability on your part. You are therefore invited to attend a formal performance review meeting on . . . . *(insert date - which should be at least three days after the date of the letter)* at . . . . *(insert time)* at . . . . *(insert location)*.

In the Company's opinion, you are [currently/still] failing to perform to the Company's required standards in the following respects:

- *(List each of the employee's failings in full detail and set these against the required standards of performance.)*

For your information, copies of the following documents, which support the Company's opinion, are enclosed:

- *(List copies of any supporting documentary evidence that you intend to produce and rely on at the meeting.)*

[The purpose of the meeting is to establish why you are not performing properly and what assistance, if any, the Company can offer to improve your performance. The Company will therefore consider whether you are being trained and supervised properly, whether you have the proper equipment and facilities to enable you to work to your maximum potential and whether you are fully aware of what the Company requires of you.]

OR

[The purpose of the meeting is to establish why you are still not performing properly despite two previous poor performance warnings and why the measures taken so far have not led to the required improvement. The Company will also consider whether there are any further steps that could reasonably be taken to rectify your poor performance, whether there is any reasonable likelihood of the required standards of performance being met within an acceptable time-frame and whether there is any practical alternative to dismissal, such as redeployment to any suitable alternative job.]

At the meeting, you will be given an opportunity to explain your position and to put forward any mitigating factors that you consider relevant to your case.

The meeting will be chaired by . . . . *(insert name)*, and . . . . *(insert name)* will also be present to take an attendance note of the meeting.

You have the statutory right to be accompanied at the meeting. Your companion may be either a work colleague or a trade union official of your choice. Your companion will be permitted both to address the meeting (but not to answer questions on your behalf) and to confer with you during the meeting. You should inform the chair of the meeting in advance of the identity of your chosen companion.

[We must inform you that the outcome of this meeting could result in a performance warning being issued.]

OR

(Where the employee already has an active final poor performance warning on file:) [As you already have an active final poor performance warning on your personnel file, we must inform you that the outcome of this meeting could result in your dismissal.]

If you or your chosen companion is unable to attend this meeting, you are asked to contact . . . . *(insert name)* as a matter of urgency so that an alternative date and time can be scheduled. You should take all reasonable steps to attend the meeting. Failure to attend without good reason could result in the meeting being held, and a decision being taken on your performance, in your absence.

After the meeting, you will be informed in writing of the Company's decision.

Yours sincerely

. . . .

For and on behalf of the Company

Encs

WARNING OF POOR PERFORMANCE

Date .... *(insert date)*

Dear .... *(insert name of employee)*

Further to your performance review meeting on .... *(insert date)*, this letter confirms the points agreed at that meeting. A copy of this [final] warning of poor performance will be placed on your personnel file.

At the meeting you were given the statutory right to be accompanied and you chose to (waive this right/have in attendance .... *(insert name of trade union official or work colleague)*).

We discussed the following areas of your current performance where the Company is of the opinion that you are failing to meet the required and notified standards:

- *(Summary of performance issues discussed.)*

In explaining your downturn in performance, you raised the following points:

- *(Summary of points raised by employee.)*

You now need to improve your performance in the following ways:

- *(List how employee needs to improve their performance in relation to each of the areas where they are failing to meet the required standards.)*

The Company would also like to offer you the following (internal/external) training: . ... *(list training to be given)*. If you think there are additional ways in which we can help you to improve your performance, please speak to (insert name).

The Company is prepared to allow you a [further] period to improve of (three/six) months commencing on .... *(insert date)*. During this period, we will meet with you on a (fortnightly/monthly) basis to review your performance and to discuss what, if any, progress or improvement you have made.

If you fail to make sufficient progress, you will be advised of this fact and details will be provided to you. We must also warn you that failure to reach the required standards by the end of the (three/six) month period is likely to result in further formal action being taken. The consequences could be [a final warning of poor performance] [your dismissal on the ground of poor work performance].

(Where the employee is being issued with a final warning of poor performance:) [Prior to any dismissal decision, the Company will of course give consideration to offering you any suitable alternative employment within your capabilities.]

We hope that you will work with the Company to improve your performance so that further action will not be necessary.

You have the right to appeal against the Company's decision if you are not satisfied with it. If you do wish to appeal, you must inform the Company in writing in accordance with the Company's capability procedure, a copy of which is attached for your information. If you do appeal, the Company will then invite you to attend an appeal meeting which you must take all reasonable steps to attend.

Meeting conducted by: . . . .

Yours sincerely

. . . .

For and on behalf of the Company

N.B. The letter should be signed by the person who conducted the performance review meeting whenever possible.

Please sign and return a copy of this letter to indicate that you have received it and understand its contents.

Signed: . . . . *(insert name of employee)*

Date: . . . . *(insert date)*

NOTIFICATION OF POTENTIAL DISMISSAL MEETING

Date . . . . *(insert date of letter)*

Dear . . . . *(insert name of employee)*

I am writing to advise you that, unfortunately, the Company is considering dismissing you because of the following aspects of your current (performance/conduct):

- *(List aspects of poor performance / conduct which have given rise to the proposal to dismiss the employee.)*

However, before a decision is taken by the Company, you are invited to attend a meeting on . . . . *(insert date)* at . . . . . *(insert time)* at . . . . *(insert location)* where the proposal to dismiss you will be discussed further.

For your information, copies of the following documents are enclosed:

- *(List copies of all witness statements and any other supporting documentary evidence that the employer intends to produce and rely on at the meeting.)*

These documents form the basis for the Company's complaint(s) and the Company will therefore rely on these documents in support of the proposal to dismiss you.

If you would like to submit a written statement for consideration in advance of the meeting you may do so. This should be forwarded to . . . . *(insert contact name)*. At the meeting, you will be given the full opportunity to explain your case. You may also put forward any mitigating factors which you consider relevant to your case.

The meeting will be chaired by . . . . *(insert name)*.

You have the right to be accompanied at the meeting. Your companion may be either a work colleague or a trade union official of your choice. Your companion will be permitted to address the meeting and to confer with you during the meeting but they will not be permitted to answer questions on your behalf. You should inform the chair of the meeting in advance of the identity of your chosen companion.

If you are unable to attend this meeting, you are asked to contact . . . . *(insert contact name)* as a matter of urgency so that an alternative date and time can be scheduled. You should take all reasonable steps to attend the meeting. Failure to attend without good reason could result in the meeting being held, and a decision being taken, in your absence.

After the meeting, you will be informed in writing of the Company's decision.

Yours sincerely

. . . .

(Insert signature and name of author)

DISMISSAL ON NOTICE DUE TO UNSATISFACTORY PERFORMANCE/CONDUCT LETTER

Date . . . . *(insert date of letter)*

Dear . . . . *(insert name of employee)*

[We refer to the meeting held on . . . . . . *(insert date)* regarding the Company's proposal to dismiss you.]

Having reviewed your (performance/conduct), we must now advise you that the Company has decided to terminate your employment for the following reasons:

- *(List reasons for dismissal, which should relate to the employee's conduct or performance.)*

The Company is of the view that you have not attained the standards that it expects from employees at your level.

You are entitled to receive . . . . . *(insert number) (weeks / months)* notice of termination of your employment. You (are/are not) required to work out your notice period. We therefore confirm that your date of termination will be . . . . . *(insert date)*.

You will receive your P45 in due course and you will be paid the following:

- your normal salary up to the date of the termination of your employment
- a payment in lieu of your notice period since we do not require you to work out this period*
- a sum in respect of accrued but untaken annual leave entitlement.*

*(*Delete as appropriate.)*

Please note that in accordance with your contract of employment, the Company reserves the right to deduct from your final termination payment a sum in respect of any annual leave taken in excess of your accrued entitlement as at your termination date.

[You may, if you wish, appeal against the Company's decision if you are not satisfied with it. If you do wish to appeal, you must inform . . . . *(insert name of contact)* in writing within five working days of receiving this decision. If you do appeal, you will then be invited to attend an appeal meeting which you must take all reasonable steps to attend.]

Yours sincerely

. . . .

(Insert signature and name of author)

Enc

DISMISSAL WITH NOTICE LETTER (MISCONDUCT)

Date . . . . *(insert date)*

Dear . . . . *(insert name of employee)*

Further to your disciplinary hearing on . . . . . *(insert date)* regarding . . . . *(insert details of incident)* on . . . . . . *(insert date of incident)*, this letter confirms the termination of your contract of employment. You are entitled to receive . . . . . . *(insert number) (weeks / months)* notice. You (are/are not) required to work out this notice period. We therefore confirm that the effective date of termination of your employment will be . . . . *(insert date)*.

At the hearing you were given the statutory right to be accompanied and you chose to (waive this right/ have in attendance . . . . *(insert name of trade union official or work colleague)*).

A full investigation of the facts surrounding the complaint against you was made by . . . . *(insert name)*. Having put the specific facts to you for your comment at the disciplinary hearing, it was decided that your explanation/excuses were not acceptable. For this reason, and in consideration of a previous active final written warning you received for similar misconduct, the Company believes it is left with no alternative but to dismiss you with notice on the ground of misconduct. The Company would refer you to the following aspects of your conduct which are, in the Company's view, unacceptable and which have led to your dismissal:

- *(List each of the complaints which have resulted in the employee's dismissal.)*

You will receive your P45 in due course and you will be paid the following:

- your normal salary up to the date of the termination of your employment
- a payment in lieu of your notice period since we do not require you to work out this period*
- a sum in respect of accrued but untaken annual leave entitlement*.

*(*Delete as appropriate)*

Please note that in accordance with your contract of employment, the Company reserves the right to deduct from your final termination payment a sum in respect of any annual leave taken in excess of your accrued entitlement as at your termination date.

You have the right to appeal against the Company's decision if you are not satisfied with it. If you do wish to appeal, you must inform the Company in writing in accordance with the Company's disciplinary procedure, a copy of which is attached for your information.

If you do appeal, the Company will then invite you to attend an appeal hearing which you must take all reasonable steps to attend.

Hearing conducted by: . . . . *(insert name)*

Yours sincerely

. . . .

For and on behalf of the Company

N.B. The letter confirming termination should be signed by the person who conducted the disciplinary hearing wherever possible.

NOTICE OF DISCIPLINARY APPEAL HEARING

Date . . . . *(insert date)*

Dear . . . . *(insert name of employee)*

We refer to your letter dated . . . . *(insert date)* in which you lodged an appeal against the (written warning/final written warning/termination of your contract of employment) confirmed to you in our letter dated . . . . *(insert date)*.

Your appeal against our disciplinary decision will be heard at an appeal hearing to take place on. . . . . *(insert date)* at . . . . *(insert time)* at . . . . *(insert location)*. The appeal hearing will be chaired by . . . . *(insert name - an appeal should be heard by a senior manager or director not previously involved in the procedure)*.

You have the statutory right to be accompanied at the appeal hearing. Your companion may be either a work colleague or a trade union official of your choice. Your companion will be permitted to address the hearing and to confer with you during the hearing but they will not be permitted to answer questions on your behalf. You should inform the chair of the appeal hearing in advance of the identity of your chosen companion.

If you would like to submit a written statement detailing your grounds for appeal for consideration in advance of the appeal hearing, you may do so. This should be forwarded to . . . . *(insert name)*. At the appeal hearing, you will of course be given an opportunity to set out the detailed grounds for your appeal, including providing any new evidence or new facts on which you may wish to rely.

If you or your chosen companion is unable to attend this appeal hearing, you are asked to contact . . . . *(insert name of contact)* as a matter of urgency so that an alternative date and time can be scheduled. You should take all reasonable steps to attend the appeal hearing. Failure to attend without good reason could result in the hearing being held, and a decision being taken on your appeal, in your absence.

After the hearing, you will be informed in writing of the Company's decision. Please note that the decision made following this appeal hearing will be final and there will be no further right of appeal against it.

Yours sincerely

. . . .

For and on behalf of the Company

SPECIMEN AGREEMENT

Example mediation scenario

Employee "A" had an appointment with her consultant surgeon for a medical assessment in connection with gastric band surgery and asked to take the day as sick leave.

Her boss, "B", recorded A's absence as annual leave as he believed that she is morbidly obese due to laziness. It's his view that if she chooses elective surgery, rather than an exercise programme, she has no right to claim the day (or any related absence) as sick leave.

B is dismissive of A when she claims that her weight gain is due to "medical reasons" which means her surgery is necessary.

A is also upset that B has made derogatory remarks about her weight in the office environment in front of other staff. B claims it was only banter and that A is over-sensitive.

As a result of this treatment, A raised a grievance.

Rather than resorting to formal procedures both A and B have agreed to try to resolve their differences via mediation.

The process is successful and on the following page is a specimen agreement.

Note. Whilst most disputes will just involve two parties, A and B, a director or senior manager "C" may have to sign the mediation agreement as well. This usually happens where authorisation for financial compensation is necessary or, as in this example, where a senior manager has to oversee the working relationship between the parties following mediation.

AGREEMENT

Between

. . . . *(insert name of employee "A")*

and

. . . . *(insert name of employee "B")*

It is agreed that:

A's absence on October 1 2009 will be treated as sick leave; she will be credited with one day's annual leave.

A agrees to withdraw the grievance lodged against B and not to initiate any further grievances based on any dealings between them prior to today's date.

A accepts that B's belief that her absence should have been taken as annual leave was genuine, albeit mistaken in the circumstances.

A agrees to provide written evidence from her consultant concerning her forthcoming surgery to confirm that it is a medical necessity that justifies the leave as sickness absence.

B agrees that any future leave in connection with A's medical condition will be recorded as sickness absence.

B agrees that he will re-read his employer's Sickness Absence Policy for future reference.

B acknowledges that he made personal remarks about A in relation to her weight and the taking of this leave that she found upsetting.

A accepts that these remarks were only made as part of established office banter and were not meant seriously.

B agrees that he will refrain from making such remarks in the future.

A and B will review the operation of this agreement at a follow-up meeting to be held in four to six weeks' time.

In the meantime, C will monitor the working relationship between A and B on a weekly basis.

Signed at .... *(insert location)* on .... *(insert date)*

Signature .... *(insert signature of "A")*

Signature .... *(insert signature of "B")*

Confirmed on behalf of .... *(insert company name)*
by .... *(insert name of director etc.)*

MEDIATION CHECKLIST

	Y	N
1. Preparation		
Have the parties been contacted to set a date and time for the mediation?	❑	❑
Has the process been explained to both sides?	❑	❑
Has background information been obtained on the dispute?	❑	❑
Have the parties been asked to draft an opening statement for the mediation?	❑	❑
If applicable, have the relevant company policies been obtained?	❑	❑
2. Room set-up		
Is there a meeting room available that will accommodate the parties?	❑	❑
Are there two smaller meeting rooms close by?	❑	❑
If not, have alternative arrangements been made off site?	❑	❑
Are the areas sufficiently quiet and private?	❑	❑
Are the rooms clean and free of clutter?	❑	❑
Is a fax machine, printer and laptop easily accessible?	❑	❑
For the mediation session itself, are the following available:		
- pens and notepads?	❑	❑
- flipchart and marker pens?	❑	❑
- a supply of tissues?	❑	❑
- refreshments, such as tea, coffee, water and biscuits?	❑	❑
3. Mediator's opening statement - points to remember		
Thank everyone for coming.	❑	❑
Introduce the parties to each other.	❑	❑
Ask how the parties would like to be addressed, e.g. first names or surnames.	❑	❑

	Y	N
Explain the role of the mediator.	❑	❑
State that the role of mediator will involve playing Devil's Advocate.	❑	❑
Explain that mediation is voluntary and non-binding to the point of agreement.	❑	❑
State that due to confidentiality, discussions can't be referred to in any future proceedings.	❑	❑
Emphasise that no confidential information will be passed between the parties.	❑	❑
Make it clear that no tape recorders are to be used.	❑	❑
Describe how the process works, e.g. joint and private sessions.	❑	❑
Make it clear that more time may be spent with one party than the other.	❑	❑
State that each side must be allowed to speak without interruption.	❑	❑
Ask the parties if they have any questions.	❑	❑

4. Mediation process - points to remember

Don't try to solve problems for the parties unless they have run out of ideas.	❑	❑
If they do need help with solutions, only suggest those that are realistic.	❑	❑
Resist the temptation to categorise the issues and force a solution too quickly.	❑	❑
Don't get drawn into giving your personal opinion.	❑	❑
Just convey what has been said between the parties. Don't exaggerate.	❑	❑
Take regular breaks.	❑	❑
Whilst the parties control the outcome, it's the mediator who controls the process.	❑	❑

LETTER INVITING EMPLOYEE TO MEDIATION

Date .... *(insert date)*

Dear .... *(insert name of employee)*

Following our recent meeting regarding .... *(insert nature of dispute)*, I am writing to formally invite you to attend a mediation session in an attempt to resolve this/these issue(s).

As previously explained, this will involve meeting with a neutral third party mediator who will facilitate discussions with the aim of finding a mutually acceptable solution. Please be aware that mediation is purely voluntary and you will not be under any pressure at any point during the process. Mediation only becomes binding if and when a settlement agreement is drafted and signed by both parties.

Due to the nature of the issue(s), we propose that the mediator will be .... *(insert name and position)* from within the Company.

OR

Due to the nature of the issue(s), we propose to use an external mediator from .... *(insert name of company here)*. You should note that the cost of their services will be solely the Company's responsibility.

The Company does not encourage the involvement of workplace or Trade Union representatives in the mediation process. However it will consider a reasonable request to allow a workplace companion to accompany you for moral support. If you wish to bring someone with you, please confirm who this will be when replying to this letter.

We are looking to schedule the mediation session on .... *(insert date)* at .... *(insert venue)*. We propose that it will start at .... *(insert time)* and is scheduled to end at .... *(insert time)* at the latest.

Please confirm that you agree to our nominated mediator and that the proposed date is convenient.

Yours sincerely

....
For and on behalf of the Company

LETTER REQUESTING INFORMATION FROM AN EXTERNAL MEDIATOR

Date . . . . *(insert date)*

Dear . . . . *(insert name of employee)*

We wish to retain the services of an external mediator to deal with a workplace dispute that has arisen within our Company involving . . . . *(insert brief details of those involved and the issue(s)).*

To enable us to make a selection we would be obliged if you would provide us with the following information:

1. When did you qualify as a mediator?

2. What training have you undertaken?

3. What experience do you have in dealing with this type of issue?

4. What is your success rate?

5. Are you a member of any professional bodies?

6. Do you have insurance?

7. Do you have references from previous clients that you can provide?

8. On what basis do you charge for your professional services?

Finally, please may we have a copy of your terms and conditions of business, a copy of your indemnity insurance certificate and confirmation of your availability to deal with this matter and any dates that must be avoided.

Yours sincerely

. . . .
For and on behalf of the Company

MEDIATION POLICY

The ACAS Code of Practice on Discipline and Grievance Procedures came into effect on April 6 2009. It encourages the use of mediation within the workplace to resolve disputes at an early stage. The Company supports that recommendation and this Policy applies to all employees.

What is mediation?

Mediation is a voluntary process, and the company cannot force an employee to undertake it. However, whilst it is undertaken on an informal basis, any issues discussed will remain confidential. Due to its flexibility, mediation can be used in a wide range of situations. These include:

- personality clashes
- differences of opinion
- communication issues
- grievances.

It will not be used to resolve:

- disputes over contract terms
- complaints over policies
- objections to the Company fulfilling its legal obligations, e.g. health and safety compliance.

The role of the mediator

A neutral third party acts as a mediator to assist those involved in a dispute to reach an agreement that is accepted and suitable for all sides. The mediator will: **(1)** always keep matters confidential; **(2)** co-ordinate the process and facilitate the meeting(s); **(3)** encourage the parties to speak openly about the issue and express their views; **(4)** where necessary, meet with the parties individually in private; and **(5)** if necessary, suggest ways to resolve the situation.

Wherever possible, the Company will use an independent person with sufficient seniority from within the organisation to act as a mediator. Where this is not possible, it will appoint an external accredited mediator. The company shall bear their costs and the employee will not be asked to contribute to this.

The Company's decision on who will act as mediator is final.

Employees' responsibilities

Employees involved in mediation must:

- approach the process positively
- respect the views of the other parties involved
- act professionally at all times.

Formal proceedings

Mediation does not replace the Company's formal Disciplinary and Grievance Procedures and the Company reserves the right to implement these processes wherever it deems appropriate.

Workplace companions

The Company does not encourage the involvement of workplace companions, e.g. colleagues or Trade Union representatives, in the mediation process and employees have no statutory right to have them involved. Neither are family members, friends or legal representatives permitted to attend.

However, the Company does recognise that employees may wish to have a companion to accompany them for moral support. It will, therefore, not refuse an employee's reasonable request in this regard. Should an employee wish to be accompanied, they should indicate this and advise the Company of their nominated companion when agreeing the proposed date for the mediation session.

ACAS CODE OF PRACTICE

Foreword

The ACAS Code of Practice on discipline and grievance is set out at paras 1 to 45 on the following pages. It provides basic practical guidance to employers, employees and their representatives and sets out principles for handling disciplinary and grievance situations in the workplace.

The Code does not apply to dismissals due to redundancy or the non-renewal of fixed term contracts on their expiry. Guidance on handling redundancies is contained in ACAS' advisory booklet on Redundancy handling. The Code is issued under section 199 of the Trade Union and Labour Relations (Consolidation) Act 1992 and was laid before both Houses of Parliament on December 9 2008. It came into effect by order of the Secretary of State on April 6 2009 and replaces the Code issued in 2004.

A failure to follow the Code does not, in itself, make a person or organisation liable to proceedings. However, employment tribunals will take the Code into account when considering relevant cases. Tribunals will also be able to adjust any awards made in relevant cases by up to 25% for unreasonable failure to comply with any provision of the Code. This means that if the tribunal feels that an employer has unreasonably failed to follow the guidance set out in the Code they can increase any award they have made by up to 25%. Conversely, if they feel an employee has unreasonably failed to follow the guidance set out in the code they can reduce any award they have made by up to 25%.

Employers and employees should always seek to resolve disciplinary and grievance issues in the workplace. Where this is not possible employers and employees should consider using an independent third party to help resolve the problem. The third party need not come from outside the organisation but could be an internal mediator, so long as they are not involved in the disciplinary or grievance issue. In some cases, an external mediator might be appropriate.

Many potential disciplinary or grievance issues can be resolved informally. A quiet word is often all that is required to resolve an issue. However, where an issue cannot be resolved informally then it may be pursued formally. This Code sets out the basic requirements of fairness that will be applicable in most cases; it is intended to provide the standard of reasonable behaviour in most instances.

Employers would be well advised to keep a written record of any disciplinary or grievances cases they deal with.

Organisations may wish to consider dealing with issues involving bullying, harassment or whistleblowing under a separate procedure.

More comprehensive advice and guidance on dealing with disciplinary and grievance situations is contained in the ACAS booklet, "Discipline and grievances at work: the ACAS guide". The booklet also contains sample disciplinary and grievance procedures. Copies of the guidance can be obtained from ACAS.

Unlike the Code employment tribunals are not required to have regard to the ACAS guidance booklet. However, it provides more detailed advice and guidance that employers and employees will often find helpful both in general terms and in individual cases.

The Code of Practice

Introduction

1. This Code is designed to help employers, employees and their representatives deal with disciplinary and grievance situations in the workplace.

- disciplinary situations include misconduct and/or poor performance. If employers have a separate capability procedure they may prefer to address performance issues under this procedure. If so, however, the basic principles of fairness set out in this Code should still be followed, albeit that they may need to be adapted
- grievances are concerns, problems or complaints that employees raise with their employers.

The Code does not apply to redundancy dismissals or the non renewal of fixed term contracts on their expiry.

2. Fairness and transparency are promoted by developing and using rules and procedures for handling disciplinary and grievance situations. These should be set down in writing, be specific and clear. Employees and, where appropriate, their representatives should be involved in the development of rules and procedures. It is also important to help employees and managers understand what the rules and procedures are, where they can be found and how they are to be used.

3. Where some form of formal action is needed, what action is reasonable or justified will depend on all the circumstances of the particular case. Employment tribunals will take the size and resources of an employer into account when deciding on relevant cases and it may sometimes not be practicable for all employers to take all of the steps set out in this Code.

4. That said, whenever a disciplinary or grievance process is being followed it is important to deal with issues fairly. There are a number of elements to this:

- employers and employees should raise and deal with issues promptly and should not unreasonably delay meetings, decisions or confirmation of those decisions

- employers and employees should act consistently
- employers should carry out any necessary investigations, to establish the facts of the case
- employers should inform employees of the basis of the problem and give them an opportunity to put their case in response before any decisions are made
- employers should allow employees to be accompanied at any formal disciplinary or grievance meeting
- employers should allow an employee to appeal against any formal decision made.

Discipline

Keys to handling disciplinary issues in the workplace

Establish the facts of each case

5. It is important to carry out necessary investigations of potential disciplinary matters without unreasonable delay to establish the facts of the case. In some cases this will require the holding of an investigatory meeting with the employee before proceeding to any disciplinary hearing. In others, the investigatory stage will be the collation of evidence by the employer for use at any disciplinary hearing.

6. In misconduct cases, where practicable, different people should carry out the investigation and disciplinary hearing.

7. If there is an investigatory meeting this should not by itself result in any disciplinary action. Although there is no statutory right for an employee to be accompanied at a formal investigatory meeting, such a right may be allowed under an employer's own procedure.

8. In cases where a period of suspension with pay is considered necessary, this period should be as brief as possible, should be kept under review and it should be made clear that this suspension is not considered a disciplinary action.

Inform the employee of the problem

9. If it is decided that there is a disciplinary case to answer, the employee should be notified of this in writing. This notification should contain sufficient information about the alleged misconduct or poor performance and its possible consequences to enable the employee to prepare to answer the case at a disciplinary meeting. It would normally be appropriate to provide copies of any written evidence, which may include any witness statements, with the notification.

10. The notification should also give details of the time and venue for the disciplinary meeting and advise the employee of their right to be accompanied at the meeting.

Hold a meeting with the employee to discuss the problem

11. The meeting should be held without unreasonable delay whilst allowing the employee reasonable time to prepare their case.

12. Employers and employees (and their companions) should make every effort to attend the meeting. At the meeting the employer should explain the complaint against the employee and go through the evidence that has been gathered. The employee should be allowed to set out their case and answer any allegations that have been made. The employee should also be given a reasonable opportunity to ask questions, present evidence and call relevant witnesses. They should also be given an opportunity to raise points about any information provided by witnesses. Where an employer or employee intends to call relevant witnesses they should give advance notice that they intend to do this.

Allow the employee to be accompanied at the meeting

13. Workers have a statutory right to be accompanied by a companion where the disciplinary meeting could result in:

- a formal warning being issued; or
- the taking of some other disciplinary action; or
- the confirmation of a warning or some other disciplinary action (appeal hearings).

14. The chosen companion may be a fellow worker, a trade union representative, or an official employed by a trade union. A trade union representative who is not an employed official must have been certified by their union as being competent to accompany a worker.

15. To exercise the statutory right to be accompanied workers must make a reasonable request. What is reasonable will depend on the circumstances of each individual case. However, it would not normally be reasonable for workers to insist on being accompanied by a companion whose presence would prejudice the hearing nor would it be reasonable for a worker to ask to be accompanied by a companion from a remote geographical location if someone suitable and willing was available on site.

16. The companion should be allowed to address the hearing to put and sum up the worker's case, respond on behalf of the worker to any views expressed at the meeting and confer with the worker during the hearing. The companion does not, however, have the right to answer questions on the worker's behalf, address the hearing if the worker does not wish it or prevent the employer from explaining their case.

Decide on appropriate action

17. After the meeting decide whether or not disciplinary or any other action is justified and inform the employee accordingly in writing.

18. Where misconduct is confirmed or the employee is found to be performing unsatisfactorily it is usual to give the employee a written warning. A further act of misconduct or failure to improve performance within a set period would normally result in a final written warning.

19. If an employee's first misconduct or unsatisfactory performance is sufficiently serious, it may be appropriate to move directly to a final written warning. This might occur where the employee's actions have had, or are liable to have, a serious or harmful impact on the organisation.

20. A first or final written warning should set out the nature of the misconduct or poor performance and the change in behaviour or improvement in performance required (with timescale). The employee should be told how long the warning will remain current. The employee should be informed of the consequences of further misconduct, or failure to improve performance, within the set period following a final warning. For instance that it may result in dismissal or some other contractual penalty such as demotion or loss of seniority.

21. A decision to dismiss should only be taken by a manager who has the authority to do so. The employee should be informed as soon as possible of the reasons for the dismissal, the date on which the employment contract will end, the appropriate period of notice and their right of appeal.

22. Some acts, termed gross misconduct, are so serious in themselves or have such serious consequences that they may call for dismissal without notice for a first offence. But a fair disciplinary process should always be followed, before dismissing for gross misconduct.

23. Disciplinary rules should give examples of acts which the employer regards as acts of gross misconduct. These may vary according to the nature of the organisation and what it does, but might include things such as theft or fraud, physical violence, gross negligence or serious insubordination.

24. Where an employee is persistently unable or unwilling to attend a disciplinary meeting without good cause the employer should make a decision on the evidence available.

Provide employees with an opportunity to appeal

25. Where an employee feels that disciplinary action taken against them is wrong or unjust they should appeal against the decision. Appeals should be heard without unreasonable delay and ideally at an agreed time and place. Employees should let employers know the grounds for their appeal in writing.

26. The appeal should be dealt with impartially and wherever possible, by a manager who has not previously been involved in the case.

27. Workers have a statutory right to be accompanied at appeal hearings.

28. Employees should be informed in writing of the results of the appeal hearing as soon as possible.

Special cases

29. Where disciplinary action is being considered against an employee who is a trade union representative the normal disciplinary procedure should be followed. Depending on the circumstances, however, it is advisable to discuss the matter at an early stage with an official employed by the union, after obtaining the employee's agreement.

30. If an employee is charged with, or convicted of a criminal offence this is not normally in itself reason for disciplinary action. Consideration needs to be given to what effect the charge or conviction has on the employee's suitability to do the job and their relationship with their employer, work colleagues and customers.

Grievance

Keys to handling grievances in the workplace

Let the employer know the nature of the grievance

31. If it is not possible to resolve a grievance informally employees should raise the matter formally and without unreasonable delay with a manager who is not the subject of the grievance. This should be done in writing and should set out the nature of the grievance.

Hold a meeting with the employee to discuss the grievance

32. Employers should arrange for a formal meeting to be held without unreasonable delay after a grievance is received.

33. Employers, employees and their companions should make every effort to attend the meeting. Employees should be allowed to explain their grievance and how they think it should be resolved. Consideration should be given to adjourning the meeting for any investigation that may be necessary.

Allow the employee to be accompanied at the meeting

34. Workers have a statutory right to be accompanied by a companion at a grievance meeting which deals with a complaint about a duty owed by the employer to the worker. So this would apply where the complaint is, for example, that the employer is not honouring the worker's contract, or is in breach of legislation.

35. The chosen companion may be a fellow worker, a trade union representative or an official employed by a trade union. A trade union representative who is not an employed official must have been certified by their union as being competent to accompany a worker.

36. To exercise the right to be accompanied a worker must first make a reasonable request. What is reasonable will depend on the circumstances of each individual

case. However it would not normally be reasonable for workers to insist on being accompanied by a companion whose presence would prejudice the hearing nor would it be reasonable for a worker to ask to be accompanied by a companion from a remote geographical location if someone suitable and willing was available on site.

37. The companion should be allowed to address the hearing to put and sum up the worker's case, respond on behalf of the worker to any views expressed at the meeting and confer with the worker during the hearing. The companion does not however, have the right to answer questions on the worker's behalf, address the hearing if the worker does not wish it or prevent the employer from explaining their case.

Decide on appropriate action

38. Following the meeting decide on what action, if any, to take. Decisions should be communicated to the employee, in writing, without unreasonable delay and, where appropriate, should set out what action the employer intends to take to resolve the grievance. The employee should be informed that they can appeal if they are not content with the action taken.

Allow the employee to take the grievance further if not resolved

39. Where an employee feels that their grievance has not been satisfactorily resolved they should appeal. They should let their employer know the grounds for their appeal without unreasonable delay and in writing.

40. Appeals should be heard without unreasonable delay and at a time and place which should be notified to the employee in advance.

41. The appeal should be dealt with impartially and wherever possible by a manager who has not previously been involved in the case.

42. Workers have a statutory right to be accompanied at any such appeal hearing.

43. The outcome of the appeal should be communicated to the employee inwriting without unreasonable delay.

Overlapping grievance and disciplinary cases

44. Where an employee raises a grievance during a disciplinary process the disciplinary process may be temporarily suspended in order to deal with the grievance. Where the grievance and disciplinary cases are related it may be appropriate to deal with both issues concurrently.

Collective grievances

45. The provisions of this code do not apply to grievances raised on behalf of two or more employees by a representative of a recognised trade union or other appropriate workplace representative. These grievances should be handled in accordance with the organisation's collective grievance process.

COMPROMISE AGREEMENT (NOT TO BE USED WITHOUT LEGAL ADVICE)

THIS AGREEMENT is made on . . . . *(insert date)*

AND IS MADE BETWEEN:

. . . . Limited *(insert name of Company)* whose registered office is at . . . . *(insert registered office details)* ("the Company"); and

. . . . *(insert name of employee)* of . . . . *(insert address of employee)* ("the Employee")

RECITALS:

1. The Employee has been employed by the Company under the terms of a contract of employment dated . . . . *(insert date)*.

2. This Agreement satisfies the conditions regulating compromise agreements under:

- Section 203 of the **Employment Rights Act 1996**
- Section 72 of the **Race Relations Act 1976**
- Section 77 of the **Sex Discrimination Act 1975**
- Schedule 3A to the **Disability Discrimination Act 1995**
- Schedule 4 to the **Employment Equality (Religion or Belief) Regulations 2003**
- Schedule 4 to the **Employment Equality (Sexual Orientation) Regulations 2003**
- Schedule 5 to the **Employment Equality (Age) Regulations 2006**
- Regulation 9 of the **Part-Time Workers (Prevention of Less Favourable Treatment) Regulations 2000**
- Regulation 8 of the **Fixed-Term Employees (Prevention of Less Favourable Treatment) Regulations 2002**
- Regulation 35 of the **Working Time Regulations 1998**
- Section 49 of the **National Minimum Wage Act 1998**
- Section 288 of the **Trade Union and Labour Relations (Consolidation) Act 1992**.

3. The Employee has received independent legal advice from a solicitor, ... *(insert name of solicitor)* of . . . . *(insert firm name)* of . . . . *(insert firm address)*, as to the terms and effect of this Agreement and, in particular, its effect upon their ability to pursue their rights in an employment tribunal. By signing this Agreement, ... *(insert firm name)* warrants that the solicitor who provided the advice holds a current practising certificate and that the firm currently maintains the level of indemnity cover required of it by the Law Society covering the risk of a claim by the Employee in respect of any loss arising in consequence of the advice they have received.

THE COMPANY AND THE EMPLOYEE AGREE AS FOLLOWS:

1. The employment of the Employee by the Company (will terminate/terminated) on . . . . *(insert date)* ("the Termination Date").

2. This Agreement is in full and final settlement of all employment related claims that the Employee has and/or may have against the Company whether or not they are or could be in the contemplation of the parties at the time of signing this Agreement.

3. The Employee has notified the Company that they consider they are in a position to make a complaint of . . . . *(insert details of employee's complaint, for example unfair dismissal, sex discrimination, race discrimination, etc. and refer to any correspondence in which the employee has notified the Company of their complaint).*

4. Neither the Employee nor the Company shall directly or indirectly make or otherwise communicate any disparaging or derogatory statements about the other, either verbally, in writing or otherwise, which might reasonably be considered to insult, damage or impugn their reputation.

5. The Company shall:

5.1. Pay the Employee their salary up to and including the Termination Date and pay in lieu of any accrued but unused annual leave entitlement. These sums will be subject to normal statutory income tax and National Insurance deductions.

5.2. Without admission of any liability as claimed or otherwise, pay to the Employee by way of compensation for termination of employment the sum of £ . . . . . . *(insert amount)* within 14 days of the signing of this Agreement ("the Payment"). Of this sum, £ . . . . . *(insert amount)* will be paid free of income tax and National Insurance deductions pursuant to section 401 of the Income Tax (Earnings and Pensions) Act 2003 and the balance of £ . . . . . *(insert amount)* will be paid after the deduction of income tax and National Insurance.

5.3. Pay the Employee a sum in respect of . . . . . *(insert number)* (weeks/months) pay in lieu of (contractual/statutory minimum) notice within 14 days of the signing of this Agreement ("the Pay in Lieu"). This sum will be (subject to normal statutory income tax and National Insurance deductions/paid free of income tax and National Insurance deductions as it does not represent contractual remuneration).*

5.4. Pay the Employee a statutory redundancy payment of £ . . . . *(insert amount)*, paid free of income tax and National Insurance deductions, within 14 days of the signing of this Agreement.*

5.5. Provide the Employee with a P45 within 14 days of the signing of this Agreement.

5.6. Continue, up to and including . . . . . . *(insert date)*, to provide the Employee with the benefits of (*life assurance, private medical insurance and pension scheme contributions) on the same terms as those benefits were provided to the Employee as at the Termination Date.*

5.7. Permit the Employee to retain their company car until . . . . *(insert date)* on the same terms and conditions as they enjoyed the use of that car during their employment but on the understanding that no mileage incurred by the Employee will constitute travel between their home and the Company's premises nor will it constitute business travel.*

5.8. Provide the Employee with a reference in the attached terms should the same be requested by any potential employer of the Employee.*

5.9. Contribute to the Employee's legal costs in seeking advice as to the terms and effects of this Agreement up to a maximum of £ . . . . *(insert amount)* plus VAT on receipt of an appropriate invoice in the Employee's name and marked payable by the Company and which refers to the advice.*

*(*Delete as appropriate.)*

6. The Employee shall:

6.1. Not divulge to any third party at any time any trade secrets or other confidential information belonging to the Company or any of its associated companies and not use such secrets or information for their own benefit or that of any third party.

6.2. Return to the Company all documents, computer hardware and software, keys, cards and any other property which belongs to the Company or relates in any way to the business of the Company or any associated company which are in their possession or under their control.

6.3. Refrain from disclosing the contents of the terms of this Agreement other than to their spouse, partner, lawyer or accountant except as may be ordered by any court, government agency or as required by law.

6.4. Accept full responsibility for the payment of any income tax and national insurance deductions not already made by the Company and indemnify and keep indemnified the Company against all and any liabilities to income tax or National Insurance deductions which the Company may incur in respect of or by reason of the Payment or the Pay in Lieu and, within seven days of being informed by the Company of the amount of any such tax assessment, pay to the Company an equivalent amount.

6.5. Warrant as a strict condition of this Agreement that they have not at the date of this Agreement accepted, either verbally or in writing, an offer of employment or entered into a contract for services or a consultancy agreement with any person, firm or company.

6.6. Warrant as a strict condition of this Agreement that they have not knowingly committed any breach of duty to the Company, or any breach of the terms of their contract of employment, and that there are no circumstances of which they are aware or ought reasonably to be aware which would constitute a repudiatory breach on the Employee's part of any express or implied term of their contract of employment which would entitle or have entitled the Company to terminate their contract of employment without notice or payment in lieu of notice.

6.7. Resign from their directorship (and as Company Secretary) with the Company with effect from the Termination Date, execute a letter of resignation in such form as the Company shall require and execute any further documents as may be necessary to give full effect to the resignation, including completing any formalities necessary to secure the amendment of records at Companies House.

6.8. Forthwith withdraw their employment tribunal claim number . . . . *(insert number)*.

6.9. Accept the payments and actions of the Company set out above in full and final settlement of all or any claims arising out of their contract of employment or its termination which they may have against the Company or any associated company or any of its or their officers or employees, whether such claims are known or unknown to the Employee and whether or not they are or could be in the Employee's contemplation at the time of signing this Agreement, and whether such claims are contractual, statutory or otherwise, including, but not limited to, claims for:

- Damages for breach of contract (whether brought before any employment tribunal or otherwise) in respect of any salary, holiday pay, notice pay, bonus or commission due.*
- Unauthorised deduction from wages under the Employment Rights Act 1996.*
- Holiday pay under the Working Time Regulations 1998.*

- Unfair dismissal, including constructive dismissal.*
- Damages arising out of the Company's failure to deal with the Employee's grievance in accordance with the ACAS Code of Practice on Disciplinary and Grievance Procedures or the Company's grievance procedure.*
- Damages arising out of the Company's failure to deal with disciplinary action against and/or dismissal of the Employee in accordance with the ACAS Code of Practice on Disciplinary and Grievance Procedures or the Company's disciplinary procedure.*
- Detriment relating to the making of a protected disclosure under the Public Interest Disclosure Act 1998.*
- Contractual or statutory redundancy pay.*
- Discrimination by reason of sex, sexual orientation, race, religion or belief, age, disability or trade union membership or activity.*
- Victimisation or harassment in connection with sex, sexual orientation, race, religion or belief, age, disability or trade union membership or activity.*
- Equal pay.*
- Less favourable treatment on account of being a part-time worker.*
- Less favourable treatment on account of being a fixed-term employee.*
- Any claim arising out of the transfer of an undertaking under the Transfer of Undertakings (Protection of Employment) Regulations 2006.*

.... *(insert details of any other claims raised by the Employee).*

*(*Delete as appropriate.)*

6.10. Accept that if their rights under any of the provisions referred to above have not been validly and lawfully excluded by the provisions of this Agreement and if they should purport to exercise such rights (or any of them) and if an employment tribunal or other court should find that any compensation is payable to the Employee by the Company as a consequence, the monies paid to the Employee under this Agreement shall be deducted (so far as may be requisite) from any award of compensation in diminution or extinction thereof.

6.11. Accept that the Payment and the Pay in Lieu to be made by the Company pursuant to the terms of clauses 5.2 and 5.3 of this Agreement are entirely conditional on the Employee's compliance with the warranties given in clauses 6.5 and 6.6 of this Agreement.

6.12. Agree that if they materially breach any material provision of this Agreement, they will repay to the Company a sum equivalent to the Payment and/or the Pay in Lieu (after deduction of all income tax and National Insurance contributions which may be due) and that the Payment and/or the Payment in Lieu is recoverable from them by the Company as a debt.

SIGNED:

. . . .
Director

For and on behalf of the Company

SIGNED:

. . . . *(insert name of employee)*

SIGNED:

. . . . *(insert name of solicitor)*

For and on behalf of . . . . *(insert name of firm)*

EQUAL OPPORTUNITIES AND DIGNITY AT WORK POLICY

Policy statement

The Company is an equal opportunity employer and is fully committed to a policy of treating all of its employees and job applicants equally. The Company will avoid unlawful discrimination in all aspects of employment including recruitment and selection, promotion, transfer, opportunities for training, pay and benefits, other terms of employment, discipline, selection for redundancy and dismissal.

The Company will take all reasonable steps to employ, train and promote employees on the basis of their experience, abilities and qualifications without regard to age, disability, gender reassignment, marriage and civil partnership, pregnancy and maternity, race (including colour, nationality and ethnic or national origins), religion or belief, sex or sexual orientation. In this policy, these are known as the "protected characteristics".

The Company will also take all reasonable steps to provide a work environment in which all employees are treated with respect and dignity and that is free from harassment and bullying based upon age, disability, gender reassignment, race (including colour, nationality and ethnic or national origins), religion or belief, sex or sexual orientation. In this policy, these are known as the "anti-harassment protected characteristics". All employees are responsible for conducting themselves in accordance with this policy. The Company will not condone or tolerate any form of harassment, whether engaged in by employees or by outside third parties who do business with the Company, such as clients, customers, contractors and suppliers.

Employees have a duty to co-operate with the Company to make sure that this policy is effective in ensuring equal opportunities and in preventing discrimination, harassment or bullying. Action will be taken under the Company's disciplinary procedure against any employee who is found to have committed an act of improper or unlawful discrimination, harassment, bullying or intimidation. Serious breaches of this equal opportunities and dignity at work statement will be treated as potential gross misconduct and could render the employee liable to summary dismissal. Employees should also bear in mind that they can be held personally liable for any act of unlawful discrimination or harassment. Employees who commit serious acts of harassment may also be guilty of a criminal offence.

You should draw the attention of your line manager to suspected discriminatory acts or practices or suspected cases of harassment or bullying. You must not victimise or retaliate against an employee who has made allegations or complaints of discrimination or harassment or who has provided information about such discrimination or harassment. Such behaviour will be treated as potential gross misconduct in accordance with the Company's disciplinary procedure. You should support colleagues who suffer such treatment and are making a complaint.

The Company will also take appropriate action against any third parties who are found to have committed an act of improper or unlawful harassment against its employees.

Direct discrimination

Direct discrimination occurs when, because of one of the protected characteristics, a job applicant or an employee is treated less favourably than other job applicants or employees are treated or would be treated.

The treatment will still amount to direct discrimination even if it is based on the protected characteristic of a third party with whom the job applicant or employee is associated and not on the job applicant's or employee's own protected characteristic. In addition, it can include cases where it is perceived that a job applicant or an employee has a particular protected characteristic when in fact they do not.

The Company will take all reasonable steps to eliminate direct discrimination in all aspects of employment.

Indirect discrimination

Indirect discrimination is treatment that may be equal in the sense that it applies to all job applicants or employees but which is discriminatory in its effect on, for example, one particular sex or racial group.

Indirect discrimination occurs when there is applied to the job applicant or employee a provision, criterion or practice (PCP) which is discriminatory in relation to a protected characteristic of the job applicant's or employee's. A PCP is discriminatory in relation to a protected characteristic of the job applicant's or employee's if:

- it is applied, or would be applied, to persons with whom the job applicant or employee does not share the protected characteristic
- the PCP puts, or would put, persons with whom the job applicant or employee shares the protected characteristic at a particular disadvantage when compared with persons with whom the job applicant or employee does not share it
- it puts, or would put, the job applicant or employee at that disadvantage, and
- it cannot be shown by the Company to be a proportionate means of achieving a legitimate aim.

The Company will take all reasonable steps to eliminate indirect discrimination in all aspects of employment.

Recruitment, advertising and selection

The recruitment process will be conducted in such a way as to result in the selection of the most suitable person for the job in terms of relevant experience, abilities and qualifications. The Company is committed to applying its equal opportunities policy statement at all stages of recruitment and selection.

Advertisements will aim to positively encourage applications from all suitably qualified and experienced people. When advertising job vacancies, in order to attract applications from all sections of the community, the Company will, as far as reasonably practicable:

1. Ensure advertisements are not confined to those areas or publications which would exclude or disproportionately reduce the numbers of applicants with a particular protected characteristic.
2. Avoid setting any unnecessary provisions or criteria which would exclude a higher proportion of applicants with a particular protected characteristic.

Where vacancies may be filled by promotion or transfer, they will be published to all eligible employees in such a way that they do not restrict applications from employees with a particular protected characteristic.

However, where, having regard to the nature and context of the work, having a particular protected characteristic is an occupational requirement and that occupational requirement is a proportionate means of achieving a legitimate aim, the Company will apply that requirement to the job role and this may therefore be specified in the advertisement.

The selection process will be carried out consistently for all jobs at all levels. All applications will be processed in the same way. The staff responsible for short-listing, interviewing and selecting candidates will be clearly informed of the selection criteria and of the need for their consistent application. Person specifications and job descriptions will be limited to those requirements that are necessary for the effective performance of the job. Wherever possible, all applicants will be interviewed by at least two interviewers and all questions asked of the applicants will relate to the requirements of the job. The selection of new staff will be based on the job requirements and the individual's suitability and ability to do, or to train for, the job in question.

With disabled job applicants, the Company will have regard to its duty to make reasonable adjustments to work provisions, criteria and practices or to physical features of work premises or to provide auxiliary aids or services in order to ensure that the disabled person is not placed at a substantial disadvantage in comparison with persons who are not disabled.

If it is necessary to assess whether personal circumstances will affect the performance of the job (for example, if the job involves unsociable hours or extensive travel), this will be discussed objectively, without detailed questions based on assumptions about any of the protected characteristics.

Training and promotion

The Company will train all line managers in the Company's policy on equal opportunities and in helping them identify and deal effectively with discriminatory acts or practices or acts of harassment or bullying. Line managers will be responsible for ensuring they actively promote equal opportunity within the departments for which they are responsible.

The Company will also provide training to all employees to help them understand their rights and responsibilities in relation to equal opportunities and dignity at work and what they can do to create a work environment that is free from discrimination, bullying and harassment.

Where a promotional system is in operation, it will not be discriminatory and it will be checked from time to time to assess how it is working in practice. When a group of workers who predominantly have a particular protected characteristic appear to be excluded from access to promotion, transfer and training and to other benefits, the promotional system will be reviewed to ensure there is no unlawful discrimination.

Terms of employment, benefits, facilities and services

All terms of employment, benefits, facilities and service will be reviewed from time to time, in order to ensure that there is no unlawful direct or indirect discrimination because of one or more of the protected characteristics.

Equal pay

The Company is committed to equal pay in employment. It believes its male and female employees should receive equal pay for like work, work rated as equivalent or work of equal value. In order to achieve this, the Company will endeavour to maintain a pay system that is transparent, free from bias and based on objective criteria.

Bullying and harassment

This policy covers bullying and harassment in the workplace and in any work-related setting outside the workplace, for example, during business trips and at work-related social events.

Bullying is offensive or intimidating behaviour or an abuse or misuse of power which undermines or humiliates an employee.

An employee harasses another employee if they engage in unwanted conduct related to an anti-harassment protected characteristic, and the conduct has the purpose or effect of violating the other employee's dignity, or creating an intimidating, hostile, degrading, humiliating or offensive environment for that other employee.

An employee also harasses another employee if they engage in unwanted conduct of a sexual nature, and the conduct has the purpose or effect of violating the other employee's dignity, or creating an intimidating, hostile, degrading, humiliating or offensive environment for that other employee.

Finally, an employee harasses another employee if they or a third party engage in unwanted conduct of a sexual nature or that is related to gender reassignment or sex, the conduct has the purpose or effect of violating the other employee's dignity, or creating an intimidating, hostile, degrading, humiliating or offensive environment for that other employee, and because of that other employee's rejection of or submission to the conduct, they treat that other employee less favourably than they would treat them if they had not rejected, or submitted to, the conduct.

The unwanted conduct will still amount to harassment if it is based on the anti-harassment protected characteristic of a third party with whom the employee is associated and not on the employee's own anti-harassment protected characteristic, or if it was directed at someone other than the employee, or even at nobody in particular, but they witnessed it. In addition, harassment can include cases where the unwanted conduct occurs because it is perceived that an employee has a particular anti-harassment protected characteristic, when in fact they do not.

Conduct may be harassment whether or not the person intended to offend. Something intended as a "joke" or as "office banter" may offend another person. This is because different employees find different levels of behaviour acceptable and everyone has the right to decide for themselves what behaviour they find acceptable to them.

Behaviour which a reasonable person would realise would be likely to offend an employee will always constitute harassment without the need for the employee having to make it clear that such behaviour is unacceptable, for example, touching someone in a sexual way. With other forms of behaviour, it may not always be clear in advance that it will offend a particular employee, for example, office banter and jokes. In these cases, the behaviour will constitute harassment if the conduct continues after the employee has made it clear, by words or conduct, that such behaviour is unacceptable to him or her. A single incident can amount to harassment if it is sufficiently serious.

Examples

Bullying and harassment may be verbal, non-verbal, written or physical. Examples of unacceptable behaviour include, but are not limited to, the following:

- unwelcome sexual advances, requests for sexual favours, other conduct of a sexual nature
- subjection to obscene or other sexually suggestive or racist comments or gestures, or other derogatory comments or gestures related to an anti-harassment protected characteristic
- the offer of rewards for going along with sexual advances or threats for rejecting sexual advances
- jokes or pictures of a sexual, sexist or racial nature or which are otherwise derogatory in relation to an anti-harassment protected characteristic
- demeaning comments about an employee's appearance
- questions about an employee's sex life
- the use of nick names related to an anti-harassment protected characteristic

- picking on or ridiculing an employee because of an anti-harassment protected characteristic
- isolating an employee or excluding him or her from social activities or relevant work-related matters because of an anti-harassment protected characteristic.

Reporting complaints

All allegations of discrimination or harassment will be dealt with seriously, confidentially and speedily. The Company will not ignore or treat lightly grievances or complaints of discrimination or harassment from employees.

If you wish to make a complaint of discrimination, you should use the Company's grievance procedure.

With cases of harassment, while the Company encourages employees who believe they are being harassed or bullied to notify the offender (by words or by conduct) that his or her behaviour is unwelcome, the Company also recognises that actual or perceived power and status disparities may make such confrontation impractical. In the event that such informal direct communication is either ineffective or impractical, or the situation is too serious to be dealt with informally, you should follow the procedure set out below.

If you wish to make a complaint of harassment, whether against a fellow employee or a third party, such as a client, customer, contractor or supplier, you should follow the following steps:

1. First of all, report the incident of harassment to your line manager. If you do not wish to speak to your line manager, you can instead speak to an alternative manager or to a member of the Human Resources Department.
2. Such reports should be made promptly so that investigation may proceed and any action taken expeditiously.
3. All allegations of harassment will be taken seriously. The allegation will be promptly investigated and, as part of the investigatory process, you will be interviewed and asked to provide a written witness statement setting out the details of your complaint. Confidentiality will be maintained during the investigatory process to the extent that this is practical and appropriate in the circumstances. However, in order to effectively investigate an allegation, the Company must be able to determine the scope of the investigation and the individuals who should be informed of or interviewed about the allegation. For example, the identity of the complainant and the nature of the allegations must be revealed to the alleged harasser so that he or she is able to fairly respond to the allegations. The Company reserves the right to arrange for another manager to conduct the investigation other than the manager with whom you raised the matter.

4. Once the investigation has been completed, you will be informed in writing of the outcome and the Company's conclusions and decision as soon as possible. The Company is committed to taking appropriate action with respect to all complaints of harassment which are upheld. If appropriate, disciplinary proceedings will be brought against the alleged harasser.

5. You will not be penalised for raising a complaint, even if it is not upheld, unless your complaint was both untrue and made in bad faith.

6. If your complaint is upheld and the harasser remains in the Company's employment, the Company will take all reasonable steps to ensure that you do not have to continue working alongside him or her if you do not wish to do so. The Company will discuss the options with you.

7. If your complaint is not upheld, arrangements will be made for you and the alleged harasser to continue or resume working and to repair working relationships.

Alternatively, you may, if you wish, use the Company's grievance procedure to make a complaint of harassment.

Any employee who is found to have discriminated against or harassed another employee in violation of this policy will be subject to disciplinary action under the Company's disciplinary procedure. Such behaviour may be treated as gross misconduct and could render the employee liable to summary dismissal. In addition, line managers who had knowledge that such discrimination or harassment had occurred in their departments but who had taken no action to eliminate it will also be subject to disciplinary action under the Company's disciplinary procedure.

Monitoring equal opportunity and dignity at work

The Company will regularly monitor the effects of selection decisions and personnel and pay practices and procedures in order to assess whether equal opportunity and dignity at work are being achieved. This will also involve considering any possible indirectly discriminatory effects of its working practices. If changes are required, the Company will implement them. The Company will also make reasonable adjustments to its standard working practices to overcome substantial disadvantages caused by disability.

JOB DESCRIPTION

Job title *(insert the name by which the job is usually known):*

. . . .

Department *(insert the section of the Company where the post holder will be working):*

. . . .

Responsible to *(insert the job title of the line manager of this post):*

. . . .

Responsible for *(insert the job titles of any staff to be supervised by the post holder):*

. . . .

Job purpose *(insert a brief description of the role that this position covers):*

. . . .

Main duties *(insert a list of the main job duties. List and number them in order of importance):*

. . . .

. . . .

. . . .

Additional duties *(insert a list of other duties that the post holder may be required to undertake from time to time):*

. . . .

. . . .

. . . .

Main responsibilities *(insert a list of the post holder's responsibilities, including any delegated authority they may have):*

. . . .

. . . .

. . . .

Prepared by *(insert the name and job title of the person who prepared the job description):*

. . . .

Date *(insert the date for future reference):*

. . . .

The Company reserves the right to vary or amend the duties and responsibilities of the post holder at any time according to the needs of the Company's business.

PERSON SPECIFICATION

Qualities	Essential	Desirable
Educational attainments	❑	❑
General education equivalent to	❑	❑
Knowledge and experience		
Knowledge of	❑	❑
Understanding of	❑	❑
Experience in	❑	❑
General intelligence		
Tests	❑	❑
General reasoning ability	❑	❑
Skills and special aptitudes		
Mechanical	❑	❑
Manual dexterity	❑	❑
Skill with words	❑	❑
Skill with numbers	❑	❑
Ability to	❑	❑
Artistic ability	❑	❑
Musical ability	❑	❑
Interests		
Intellectual	❑	❑
Practical/constructional	❑	❑
Physically active	❑	❑
Community	❑	❑

Disposition and personal qualities	**Essential**	**Desirable**
Reliability	❏	❏
Stability	❏	❏
Discretion and diplomacy	❏	❏
Leadership	❏	❏
Impartiality of judgment	❏	❏
Self-reliance and self-motivation	❏	❏
Circumstances		
Mobility	❏	❏
Domicile	❏	❏

Date: ....

Prepared by: ....

SAMPLE FORM COT3

Between John Bloggs ("the Claimant") v ABC Limited ("the Respondent")

Case Number: . . . . ("the Proceedings")

Withdrawal and settlement of claims reached as a result of conciliation action.

The parties have agreed as follows:

1. The Claimant will withdraw and abandon his employment tribunal Proceedings in full with effect from the date of this Agreement by sending a Notice of Withdrawal ("the Notice") by e-mail to the Happytown Employment Tribunal.
2. The Claimant agrees that he will send a copy the Notice to the Respondent's representative.
3. The parties confirm their understanding and agreement that the Proceedings will, following withdrawal of the claim by the Claimant, be dismissed by the tribunal.
4. The Respondent will pay to the Claimant, without any admission of liability, the sum of £5,000 (the "Settlement Sum") in compensation for loss of his employment. The parties believe the Settlement Sum to be a termination payment within ss.401-403 Income Taxes (Earnings and Pensions) Act 2003, but the Respondent gives no warranty to that effect. The Claimant undertakes to indemnify the Respondent in respect of any tax charged on the Settlement Sum.
5. The Settlement Sum will be paid to the Claimant within 14 days of both the receipt of **(1)** this Agreement duly signed by Claimant; and **(2)** a copy of the Notice referred to at Clause 1 of thisAgreement.
6. The terms of this Agreement are accepted by the Claimant in full and final settlement of the Proceedings and of all other claims that he has, or may have, against the Respondent or any of its current or former officers or employees arising out of his employment with the Respondent or its termination.
7. Any claims in relation to either: (i) personal injury arising otherwise than from the termination of the Claimant's employment and/or (ii) accrued pension entitlements are excluded from this Agreement. For the avoidance of doubt, the Claimant warrants that he does not have any claim for personal injury against the Respondent or any of its current or former officers or employees.

8. The Claimant agrees that with the exception of his legal advisors, his immediate family, or save as required by law that he will keep both the facts relating the Proceedings and contents of this Agreement confidential and that he will not disclose them to any other third party.

9. The parties agree that they will each bear their own costs in relation to the Proceedings and to this Agreement and that no party shall make any application for costs.

Claimant:

Signed ....

Dated ....

Respondent:

Signed ....

Dated ....

SCHEDULE 1

Withdrawal notification to be sent to the Happytown Employment Tribunal by e-mail

Subject: Notice of withdrawal of claim

Dear Sirs

John Bloggs v ABC Limited

Case Number: . . . .

In accordance with rule 25 of schedule 1 to the Employment Tribunals (Constitution and Rules of Procedure) Regulations 2004 ("the Regulations") I hereby confirm that I wish to withdraw the claim set out above in its entirety with immediate effect.

In accordance with rule 25A(1) of Schedule 1 to the Regulations, I also confirm my understanding that these Proceedings will, following withdrawal of my claim, be dismissed and that I do not object to any application by the Respondent to have the claim against it dismissed under rule 25(4) of the Regulations, if that is deemed appropriate by the tribunal.

I confirm that there will be no application for costs against the Respondent.

Yours sincerely

Mr J Bloggs

cc the Respondent's representatives (by e-mail)

SAMPLE WITNESS STATEMENT

Case number . . . .

IN THE HAPPYTOWN EMPLOYMENT TRIBUNAL

BETWEEN

Mr J Bloggs **Claimant**

and

ABC Limited **Respondent**

Statement of evidence of Mr Fred Smith

I, Fred Smith, Area Manager, of, ABC Limited, 123 High Street, Happytown,

WILL SAY:

1. At the relevant time I was the Area Manager of ABC Limited.

2. Mr Bloggs came to see me about the beginning of January and asked me if I knew about an envelope which had been placed on a notice board with a derogatory racial comment written on it.

3. I told him that I had been made aware of this by staff in the works office and had already spoken to Andy Mann our Clerical Manager who is the person responsible for keeping the notice board up-to-date. I was quite confident it would have been him due to his long service and the position of trust which he occupies.

4. I told Mr Bloggs that the Company would be making enquiries of the people in each shift that would have been in that part of the works nearest to the notice board.

5. I also said that I would personally scrutinise all personnel records to see if I could identify any similar handwriting. This I subsequently did but without success.

6. Mr Bloggs then demanded that the Company bring in a handwriting expert but this was not possible as we could not allow access to confidential records to an outside person. Plus we cannot compel members of the workforce to provide a sample of writing. To have simply asked everyone to provide one voluntarily would have met with blank refusals.

7. I meant to get back to Mr Bloggs about all of this but very soon after we embarked on a reorganisation of the Company and this occupied a great deal of my time. Consequently, and it slipped my mind.

8. If he had been concerned about this, I would have expected him to come and see me as he has never been reluctant to do so in the past.

I make this statement believing the content to be true to the best of my knowledge and belief.

Signed ....

Dated ....

Notes

Notes

Notes

Notes

Notes

Notes

Notes